NO REGRETS

Minnesota Women and the
Joan Growe Senatorial Campaign

BARBARA STUHLER

Foreword by Arvonne Fraser
Afterword by Joan Growe

The Braemar Press • St. Paul, Minnesota

Library of Congress Cataloging-in-Publication Data

Stuhler, Barbara.
No regrets.

Includes index.
1. Electioneering — Minnesota — Case studies.
2. Campaign management — Minnesota — Case studies.
3. Women in Politics — Minnesota — Case studies.
4. Growe, Joan Anderson. I. Title
JK6195.S78   1986   324.7'09776.   86-70977
ISBN 0-9616791-0-7

To
Joan Growe
and the many thousands
who built the
Minnesota's Groweing Pyramid

About the author . . .

Barbara Stuhler is an Associate Dean of Continuing Education and Extension at the University of Minnesota. She is also the author of *Ten Men of Minnesota and American Foreign Policy* and co-editor, with Gretchen Kreuter, of *Women of Minnesota: Selected Biographical Essays*, both published by the Minnesota Historical Society. She confesses to a lively interest in Minnesota politics — an interest that prompted her participation as a member of Minnesota's Groweing Steering Committee and in telling this tale of that experience.

About the contributors . . .

Arvonne Fraser is Senior Fellow and Director of the Women, Public Policy and Development project at the Hubert H. Humphrey Institute of Public Affairs, University of Minnesota. Her activities and accomplishments are legendary, and it is for good reason that she has been called "the Twin Cities' best-known and most durable feminist."

Joan Growe is Secretary of State and was the Democratic-Farmer-Labor candidate for U.S. Senator from Minnesota in 1984. Her prior victories at the polls have made her a model for other women seeking public office. She is a woman of conviction, compassion, and good humor, and, by her example, she has demonstrated that there can be victories even in defeat. Minnesota women will long remember Joan Growe's achievements and, one day, some Minnesota woman will walk through the Senate door that she opened in 1984.

Contents

Acknowledgments

THIS BOOK WOULD NOT have been written had it not been for Joan Growe's decision to run for the U.S. Senate and had it not been for the extraordinary response of women of Minnesota to the idea and organization of Minnesota's Groweing. Many men also signed up and, for that participation, they deserve a special recognition. Their enthusiastic support of a woman candidate for high public office is a good sign for the future of American politics.

When the thought of this book began to emerge, Linda Holstein and Jean West, members of Minnesota's Groweing Steering Committee, were indispensable to the process. They spent time with me in collective recall and in putting down on paper some of their recollections and their own experiences. I cannot thank them enough. All the members of the Steering Committee read the first draft and, at a meeting on September 23, 1985, they were both critical and kind, providing me with useful suggestions and improvements.

There were others who were equally generous with their time, insights, and contributions — Andrea Christianson and Elaine Voss of the Growe Campaign organization, Arvonne Fraser, Director of the Center for Women and Public

viii   ACKNOWLEDGMENTS

Policy at the University of Minnesota's Humphrey Institute of Public Affairs, and, of course, Joan Growe. Jean A. Brookins, Assistant Director for Publications and Research of the Minnesota Historical Society, was especially helpful with her counsel on how to "build" this book.

I would also like to thank the University of Minnesota for giving me a leave of absence (albeit without pay) and Harold A. Miller, Dean of Continuing Education and Extension, who approved that leave application, giving me the time to finish putting this all together.

Finally, a word of appreciation to my colleagues and friends in education, politics, and community affairs who share my joy in striving, as Fyodor Dostoyevsky once wrote, to make us "better perhaps than we are."

Foreword

JOAN GROWE IS A LADY and a tough politician in the best
sense of both terms. Minnesota's Secretary of State and a
former state legislator, she ran for the U.S. Senate in 1984
and lost. But her campaign may go down in Minnesota history as a turning point. The first woman in this state to be
endorsed by a major political party to run for U.S. Senate,
she won a primary against a maverick politican whose
name was supposed to be electorally magic. Her endorsement at the historic 1984 Democratic-Farmer-Labor party
convention took place after delegates defied party leaders
and, meeting continuously for 26 hours, selected Growe as
their nominee on the 19th ballot.

Minnesota is a state that enjoys politics and generally
considers it a respectable, if not a high, calling. We have
produced and consistently supported men and women who
have become national and even international leaders.
Hubert Humphrey is only one among many. Historically,
our politics have been clean and somewhat populist but, recently, as in much of the rest of the nation, many of our
politicians and most of the media have become political
technocrats, turning what is mainly an art into a pseudo-
science.

This is not to say that polls, demographic studies, the targeting of voters, the use of computers and other technologies in campaigns are not important. They are, but only as auxiliaries to the main task of involving citizens in a political effort and getting a majority of the voters motivated enough, emotionally committed enough, to talk positively about and vote for the candidate.

Joan Growe is a party regular, but she is female and she does not believe that party work for women should be limited to supporting male candidates and keeping the party organization going. She understands that political party endorsement in Minnesota is a required first step for those seeking major office, and, consequently, she began seeking delegates early. (Primaries are viewed in the Minnesota tradition only as checks against egregious party errors in endorsing for major offices although that tradition has been challenged more frequently in recent years. Still, primary challenges are viewed with disapproval by party regulars—the convention system of nomination being preferred.)

But political women who run for elective office are still the other, the anomaly, the exception, despite the fact that the post-suffrage women's movement has made great progress. The breadth and depth of that movement is discernible to anyone who is an astute observer, who reads between the lines or listens to the popular rhetoric. One example is that more and more women are running for office and winning, most frequently at the local level. Whether this is because women's participation at the local level has been made more acceptable by groups such as the League of Women Voters and the many female community activists over the years or whether it is because these local offices are less well paid and often volunteer jobs is something to be considered. Certainly the National Women's Political Caucus and its local affiliates have been a force for increasing women's demands and participation in politics.

In Minneapolis, the major city in Minnesota, a majority

of the city council is female, including the President of the Council, and a high proportion of its other elective offices are held by women. The current governor of the state, Rudy Perpich, chose Marlene Johnson as his running mate in 1982, after Warren Spannaus, the favored and endorsed DFL candidate, turned down Joan Growe and another woman as possible running mates and chose a farmer-legislator instead. Many believe Spannaus' error in not choosing a woman and Perpich's wisdom in picking Johnson were responsible in great part for the upset of the DFL-endorsed ticket in the primary election and the ultimate victory of the Perpich-Johnson team.

Women are in politics to stay—and not simply at the party-supporter or local elective level. Geraldine Ferraro's choice as vice presidential candidate changed the face of national politics, even though she and Mondale did not win that election. It hardly needs stating that Mondale is a Minnesotan, but it should be noted that his choice of Ferraro is given as the reason for carrying his home state by a margin of some 3,700 votes.

But the question for the future, with more and more women involved in politics and the workforce, is how politicians—female as well as male—will adapt their campaigns to motivate citizens and win elections. The baby boom generation, soon if not already a majority of the potential electorate, is a generation of two-earner families and increasing numbers of unmarried women. That generation is a product of the 60s, the civil and equal rights movements, and affluence. They are different, in the same way but also in different ways just as those of us who are their parents are different from our parents. And what is increasingly clear, with longer life spans, is that the electorate is composed of at least three generations of adults, all with different and similar sets of concerns. The objective of the politician who wants to be successful—and what politician doesn't—will have to be to compromise the needs and concerns of a very diverse constituency into a common theme and common goals. And about the only commonality among this diverse electorate in these fast changing times is their humanity.

In other words, politics today, perhaps more than ever, must revolve around people, and those people are not homogeneous. Politics is the art and science of government. Governments are instituted by people to serve people and today the word people does not mean men, with women and children as dependents. Increasingly, women are demanding to be equal partners in politics and all other aspects of life.

Joan Growe's candidacy was but one manifestation of that demand and of the strength of the women's movement. But a basic question still remains: how can women candidates for high office win and how can male and female candidates appeal to the new, and increasingly diverse, electorate?

Growe's campaign may provide some lessons.

She was successful in the endorsement contest and she was successful in the primary. She did not win the general election. (Perhaps it is worth noting here that about half the male candidates running in general elections don't win either.)

The difference in the endorsement contest was that she had more delegates than anyone else — a very simple fact — but those delegates were determined that she receive that endorsement. Growe and her campaign staff, mostly but not exclusively women, had worked for months if not years to glean those delegates. Also the DFL Feminist Caucus was the strongest and most cohesive group in that and recent DFL conventions. Labor, which has traditionally been a major force in the Democratic-Farmer-Labor (DFL) Party, had, by 1982, lost much of its political clout. Women, who long have been party activists and often the most active supporters of DFL candidates, were, by 1984 and according to party rules, half the delegates. Many of the female delegates who were not members of the DFL Feminist Caucus un-

doubtedly remembered the snub given Growe at the previous convention and their own experiences at being overlooked and overworked in party affairs.

But Growe's support among the delegates was not limited
to women. She had traveled the state, worked with and for
party leaders and activists for years, and had a strong base
of support among the farmers and "outstate" delegates attending that Convention. She led in a field of five contenders beginning with the first ballot. As the balloting
wore on and no one obtained the required majority, party
leaders gathered in caucus to try to work out a compromise.
But despite the combined efforts of the other male contenders for that nomination to reach a compromise — efforts
in which Growe ultimately participated — the delegates to
that convention rejected the advice of their leaders and insisted on an endorsement. They demanded one ballot after
another through an all-night session, taking 19 ballots before reaching the required 60 percent majority.

Growe had won the first round.

In an attempt to heal party wounds accumulated during
the endorsement and, either consciously or unconsciously,
to show that she was not just a woman's candidate, Growe
changed campaign managers after the endorsing convention. As with all campaigns, the eager and aggressive up-
coming young men moved in. She became "their candidate"
because she was the party's endorsed candidate. And most
of them came from the politics-as-science rather than
politics-as-art school, reflecting the current preoccupation
with technique and tactics and embodying the political
myths created in party headquarters and by the media,
based on superficial analyses of past campaigns and conventional male-dominated political wisdom. Essentially they
gave short shrift to the traditional party workers and the
new Growe supporters and hired outside political consul-
tants to advise them in matters of strategy, media, and polling. Whether they looked around for a consultant who had
run or could run a successful woman candidate's campaign

is unknown but can be surmised. But experienced women who tried to be helpful were rejected with little grace.

Political power is guarded assiduously, especially by young men socialized to be masters in the competitive struggle for advancement. The drive for power and position frequently leads them to overlook the fact that political power is for the purpose of governing, not for mastery in a given time and place. In any event, it was made clear to Growe's female supporters that they could raise money but that this was going to be a typical male-dominated campaign, a man's campaign with the candidate in skirts and long sleeves.

Meanwhile the media and political haunts bristled with rumors about a possible primary. No one stated it publicly, but many male party leaders and media personnel obviously thought and privately expressed the idea that the party had made an egregious mistake in endorsing a woman. Some of the defeated candidates were asked publicly whether they were considering a primary challenge, and Mark Dayton, a previous candidate for senator, toyed with the idea for a few days. The end result, as noted earlier, was that a maverick politician — Bob Mattson, son of a former public official — filed against her. The conventional wisdom was that Mattson, with his good name and patriarchal connections, might well win.

It was at this point that a small group of women, representing the views of many other women, decided that something had to be done. As Barbara Stuhler has written: "One thing was clear. There were a lot of politically interested women who were willing to commit themselves to a women's effort in the Growe campaign, but they were frustrated because no one in charge seemed willing to act upon their suggestions. It was their perception that there was little interest in a commitment to running a woman's campaign differently. Growe's convention endorsement was the product of grass-roots organizing done in large part by women. Although Growe herself never rejected women as

a resource—witness the number in key campaign posts—
nevertheless, the campaign drifted to the center and to
what many women political activists perceived as the traditional 'male' way of doing such things."

As a result, this small band of women organized the Minnesota's Groweing campaign, an independent group dedi-
cated to helping Joan Growe win that primary and, ultimately, the general election. Minnesota's Groweing was
old-fashioned, people first, organized campaigning at its
best, relying on volunteers, building a functioning pyramid
based on personal commitment, on one-to-one contacts,
combined with hard work, ingenuity and common sense.
By the time of the primary election this group had active
supporters organized and working in 283 communities outside the metropolitan area and multitudes of workers and
supporters in the metro area.

Whether Minnesota's Groweing made the crucial difference in the primary, no one will ever know. Politics is not
a science. No one factor or series of factors can ever be iso-
lated and proved with certainty. But certainly it was a major contributing factor in Growe's primary win and it
helped prove that primary challengers need more than a
father's name and a certain gender to be successful. And because primaries involve such a small percentage of the possible electorate, with only the most interested politically participating, media campaigns or gross efforts are not cost–
effective. Primaries are the important place for targeting
and this was a targeted effort.

Minnesota's Groweing, built on womens' interest in a
woman candidate and on involving interested people
directly and personally in the campaign, was something the
official campaign committee overlooked and continued to
overlook through the general election. (It should be noted
that the Mondale campaign was consistently criticized for
making the same mistake. Volunteers were asked only to
raise money and campaign events were structured as media
shows, not for the satisfaction of those attending the event.)

One could speculate about what might have happened had the regular Growe campaign taken more notice of the value of the Minnesota's Groweing effort and adopted some of its artful but simple techniques and organizational style, but the thrust of almost any campaign is determined early and is very hard to change. An overall strategy and tone is set, a plan made, staff are hired, and time is of the essence.

Likewise, it is unreasonable to expect that an independent campaign committee or a candidate herself can carry a campaign while the regular campaign organization operates on a different theory and plane.

Joan Growe and Geraldine Ferraro both lost their elections but both gained enormous respect during their campaigns. They broke barriers and created a new enthusiasm among many segments of the electorate. They may well be forerunners of a new breed of politician. Jeane Kirkpatrick, Elizabeth Dole, and Nancy Kassebaum are examples of this new breed in the Republican Party; the rejection of women as equal partners in society is a temporary right-wing phenomenon. Jeane Kirkpatrick's acceptance and popularity in the Republican Party is testimony to that fact.

And while Corazon Aquino begins to lead the Phillipines toward democracy, there is an uneasiness among the U.S. public about domestic and international policies and a yearning for new leadership. President Reagan cannot run for another term, and the male-dominated establishment finds itself caught up in the momentum of its history, institutions and political myths.

Women can provide some of the new leadership in the U.S. if they will only free themselves from the accepted tenets of political campaigning. That means daring to be different. To borrow a phrase, it means speaking in a different voice, thinking differently about political campaigns.

Women candidates are perceived to be different and the female half of the electorate is different. One of the truisms of politics is that effective candidates lead or build from their strengths, and one of women's traditional strengths is caring for and about people. Assessing women's other strengths should not be too difficult if a hard, objective look is taken at recent and past polls and elections and if new polls and demographic studies are undertaken, with experienced political women helping to analyze the data.

To argue that women are different is not to argue that they are unequal. On the face of it, the latter argument implies that men's standards are *the* standards. Rather, to argue that women are different — both in perception and reality — is to argue that both equality and practical politics require an integration of the perspectives and attributes of both sexes.

What is necessary now is a deliberate intellectual effort to shake off the conventional wisdom and the myths of recent political campaigns. What may also be useful is an objective study of the success of right-wing movements over recent decades. These groups have had a consistent theme, developed a variety of organizations, worked from the grass roots up to the top, and raised money as they raised new issues and proposed cutbacks in government. They have successfully pulled the country to the right and changed the political context, except on women's issues. The women's movement has been virtually their only opposition.

There is strength and depth in the women's movement but it has not been translated very well politically because women candidates and political activists have bought the incumbent model of campaigning. This has not been effective because there are not yet enough female incumbents — no critical mass. Women as elected officials are predominately still "the other."

But in a time when citizens are looking for new leadership and new direction, a women's perspective — common sense, pragmatism and a concern for people — could be a strength. A different voice, different messages, and different gender could be political assets rather than liabilities.

Millions of U.S. citizens do not vote. This is not out of ignorance but out of cynicism and disillusionment. A recent study indicated that registration and get-out-the vote drives have failed because people were not given a reason to vote. The connection between voting and people's lives was not made. Capturing a small percentage of the non-voting public could turn almost any election around. The right wing has done this successfully. The women's movement could do this if it concentrated its efforts and developed a nationwide network determined to change the face and dialogue of American politics.

This does not mean putting women's issues such as ERA and abortion at the top of the list in every female candidate's speech or campaign literature. These are assumed for women candidates today unless the candidate indicates otherwise. What is necessary and would be attractive to many is the posing of critical new questions, defining problems from a pragmatic, people perspective.

For example, how many people believe that nuclear arms are a key to international safety? Doesn't defense of a country include the health and welfare of its citizens? Isn't the health, education, and training of the next generation of citizens and workers an important responsibility of both parents and society? Are taxes only an evil or are they the means by which citizens finance the government programs they desire? Should public policy assume the male bread-winner model for families is the desired or normal model or should the two-earner family and the female-headed household be accepted as viable alternatives? What are the goals and objectives and the needs of a society in which three generations of adults are the citizens?

This is only the beginning of a possible list of issues for a new political dialogue. There are intelligent, effective and interested citizens — men and women alike — who recognize the world has changed and continues to change. On the international level, how do we deal with nations torn asunder by poverty, corruption, young populations and un-democratic governments? What would be an intelligent foreign policy for the oldest democracy on earth? The public supports the United Nations, according to recent polls, and worries about the place of the U.S. in world politics. Yet our students don't learn geography.

The real question is whether the women's movement will take its fair share of responsibility for leadership in this country. Leadership means taking risks, proposing new solutions to old and new problems. Being equal and secure partners in this world requires creating a new, integrated world, in which men will come to recognize and accept the nurturing skills of women as essential elements in developing amicable relationships among people.

Citizens are yearning for a chance to participate in a meaningful political dialogue. Just raising money for candidates makes politics a form of legal bribery. Women are good one-to-one communicators. The women's movement wasn't organized via the traditional media, but it's a viable movement and it's made a difference. The time has come to raise political consciousnesses and for more women to act like equal, independent citizens.

Joan Growe and Geraldine Ferraro may have been women before their time. Maybe they simply both got caught in a set of political circumstances they could not overcome. But it is also possible that the kind of campaign that the Minnesota's Groweing group ran would be a breath of fresh air in a stale political atmosphere.

Arvonne Fraser

Preface

EXCEPT FOR OCCASIONAL observations from some of the participants in this account of Minnesota's Groweing, the pronoun, "we," is used in this book. We do so because the story of Minnesota's Groweing is truly a collaborative effort. Floyd B. Olson, the distinguished if somewhat controversial governor of Minnesota, was reputed to have said that the only persons entitled to use that pronoun were editors and those with tapeworms. A witty remark, to be sure, but not entirely inclusive. This experience of ten women in organizing an independent political campaign on behalf of a woman candidate seeking election to the United States Senate in 1984 requires that pronoun.

We have chosen to write about our experience in the belief that it could be a model or guide for comparable grass-roots campaigns. We do so because, even in the days of media politics, we feel the active involvement of citizens is still relevant. We do so also in the expectation that, one day, women who constitute the majority of the population, will be equally represented in the public offices that make the decisions of this nation.

Women candidates captured public attention in 1984 even if some of the most visible ones did not win. Geraldine

Ferraro was the first woman to be the vice presidential nominee on the ticket of one of the two major parties. Even though she lost, no one can take away the euphoria that surrounded Walter Mondale's announcement of his running mate in North Oaks, Minnesota on July 12, 1984, their joint appearance in the state Capitol the following day, and the Democratic party's nomination of Ferraro by acclamation a week later on July 19 in San Francisco. There were more women candidates on the national level than ever before — 10 in Senate races and 65 contending for House seats. Only one of the Senatorial candidates, incumbent Nancy Kassebaum of Kansas, won. Nine other women who challenged incumbent Senators lost. Joan Growe was one of those nine. Only two women were newly elected to the House. Because two did not return, the net gain was zip — the number of women Representatives remained at 22.[1]

Though the losses of Ferraro, Growe, and other women candidates for national office seemed to dim the prospects for women in politics, 1984 was, in fact, a good year. A woman was elected governor of Vermont and now, with the governor of Kentucky, they number two. The first woman attorney-general was elected to that position in Rhode Island (a Republican and former nun), and 96 more women were elected to state legislatures (they now hold a total of 1,103 seats — almost 15 percent of 7,461 in all. There are five women who serve as lieutenant governors, 11 as secretaries of state, 11 as state treasurers, and five as state auditors.[2] Women now hold 13 of the top 290 leadership positions in state legislatures. In Minnesota, Independent-Republican Connie Levi of Dellwood was the choice of her party to be majority leader in the House of Representatives. More than 17,000 women — three times the number a decade ago — serve as mayors and on city councils, county commissions, and school boards.[3] Although women constitute only 10 percent of the elected political leadership in the country, they are on the rise and making their mark in American politics above and beyond what they have ever done before.[4] The city halls, courthouses, and statehouses are becoming a training ground for women political leaders, some of whom will be elected to higher office by future voters to whom gender is no object or obstacle.[5]

For the skeptics who wondered why all the fuss over a woman candidate for the United States Senate, it is because that woman took a risk for all women. Joan Growe dared to challenge an incumbent, and she proved that a woman could run a hard race, demonstrating both intelligence and stamina in the process. She dared to dream a possible dream. For women who have been excluded too long from the halls of power, Growe contested for that power. Women in all walks of life identified with her — from the battered women who have the courage to leave and say, "no more," to the women who have invaded the so-called traditional male fields of medicine, law, business, engineering, and, yes, politics. Women in many cultures and for many centuries have shared a vision of equality, recognizing that denial of women's dignity and the rejection of women's intellectual capacities serve only to diminish the human condition.[6] One day, new generations will read with awe and amazement of the time and tenacity it took for women to be accepted as equal partners in a democratic society.

It was that sense of the future that moved so many women with the nominations of Geraldine Ferraro and Joan Growe. That is why mothers took their daughters to see Ferraro. That is why so many women were energized by Growe's campaign. It was in the hope that the future might be sooner rather than later that Minnesota's Groweing was formed.

And even if Growe lost, she waged a vigorous campaign. She was direct, and she had convictions. She was tough but compassionate. She was energetic and courageous. But, like other women seeking national office in 1984, she suffered from the lack of incumbency in a year when incumbents were returned to office in striking numbers. Change in the midst of an economic boom and in a world at relative peace

was the last thing on voters' minds. Gloria Steinem, writing
of Geraldine Ferraro on election night, said, "But there is
also a sense of peace in the room. It comes from knowing
that we did our best; from knowing that Ferraro did her
best, and how very good that was."[7] We of Minnesota's
Groweing did our best. We know that Joan Growe did too;
no candidate worked harder than she did. It is, therefore,
with a good feeling and with high hopes for the future of
women in politics that we tell this story of Minnesota's
Groweing.

NO REGRETS

Minnesota Women and the
Joan Growe Senatorial Campaign

1 | The Setting

THIS IS NOT THE PLACE to tell the whole story of the campaign by Joan Growe for election to the United States Senate in 1984. It is necessary, however, to say something about Growe and her campaign in order to establish a context whereby readers can understand the rhymes and reasons for Minnesota's Groweing.

Joan Growe was no stranger to Minnesota politics. Growe's life had been, if not every woman's experience, not uncommon. Married and a mother of three sons and a daughter, she found herself some years ago having to make a fresh start as a single parent. In 1968, she returned to college earning a special education certificate from the University of Minnesota through extension classes. She worked as an elementary school teacher in the Bloomington and St. Anthony school systems and as a special education teacher at Christ Child School for Exceptional Children in St. Paul.[1] Her interest in public affairs was a product of her membership in the League of Women Voters and later of her concern as a mother over the war in Vietnam.[2] She became attracted to political life because of a desire to make an impact and to effect change.[3] In 1972, she ran as a Democratic-Farmer-Labor candidate for a House seat in the Minnesota Legislature. She won 55 percent of the vote in a 70 percent Republican district. In 1974, she ran against a popular Republican incumbent Secretary of State—Arlen Erdahl— and won, despite the prophecy of friends and colleagues that she would never make it.[4] She was reelected in 1978 when other DFL state-office holders went down to defeat and was elected again in 1982 for a third term. As Secretary of State, Joan Growe was largely responsible for changes that have established Minnesota as the state with the highest voter registration and turn-out in the country. She tended her political fences and became a highly visible and respected public figure.

It was no surprise that she was tempted by higher office.

In 1982, Growe began to think about her political options. The incumbent Independent-Republican Governor, Albert H. (Al) Quie, faced with hard recession times, had decided not to run for a second term. Warren Spannaus, the popular incumbent Attorney-General would enter the race and subsequently be endorsed by the Democratic-Farmer-Labor party. At that time with feminism and the gender gap enjoying some credibility, many were hoping that Spannaus would select a woman to be his running mate. As the only female state-wide office-holder, Joan Growe was a logical if low-key contender for Lieutenant Governor. But she, like Spannaus, was from the Twin Cities. Consequently, the DFL feminists thought their best chance for success would lie with state Representative Arlene Lehto of Duluth. Spannaus, however, chose Carl Johnson, a farmer and a 16-year House veteran whose geography, views, and personality—or so it was thought—would bring a winning balance to the ticket. Although feminists respected Spannaus, they thought he had made a strategic mistake.[5] That belief was confirmed when his primary challenger, former Governor Rudy Perpich did choose a woman as his running mate—Marlene Johnson who had strong political interests but no prior experience in public office.[6] The Perpich ticket came out on top in the primary by close to 28,000 votes and went on to win a decisive victory in the general election over the IR Wheelock Whitney-Lauris Krenik ticket by 333,308 votes.[7]

In any event, Growe had a sense that support for her might be strong enough to warrant a bid for the U.S. Senate seat in 1984. In December of 1982 she began testing the waters in earnest. Early in 1983, Bob Meek who had served in a number of capacities with various Minnesota political figures was brought in as a part-time speech writer and consultant. Elaine Voss, also an experienced political hand, came on board as Deputy Secretary of State, but she would spend evenings and weekends working on the Growe campaign. Harriett Woods of Missouri, who came close to winning a U.S. Senate seat in 1982, and her campaign manager, Jody Newman, met with Growe and her advisers to share their experience and know-how. None of this was secret — everyone expected Joan Growe would run for the Senate.[8]

On Sunday, October 2, 1983, after some months of anticipation, Joan Growe went to the Leo and Marian Fogarty farm near Belle Plaine, Minnesota to announce her candidacy for the office of U.S. Senator. She said, "I grew up in Minnesota. It's where I went to school, where I set my course. So it is here where Minnesota begins, where pioneering is a tradition that I have come to begin the greatest adventure of my public life." She articulated three themes: 1) working for peace through a nuclear freeze and reduced military spending; 2) investing in people by providing a safe environment and a good education; 3) insuring economic opportunity by supporting policies designed to achieve full employment and end discrimination. Later, Growe told reporters that she would avoid being "a woman's candidate only" but she anticipated that the gender gap would be a factor (her reference to the Equal Rights Amendment had elicited the loudest cheer on that October day). She hoped to raise between $2.5 and $3 million for her campaign, including $500,000 to win endorsement at the state convention seven months later.[9]

In the months that followed, former Governor Wendell Anderson and Congressman James Oberstar also announced their intentions to seek the Senate seat, joining Growe and Hennepin County Commissioner John Derus who had been the first to announce on August 8, 1983.

On March 20, precinct caucuses were held throughout the state. Because the primary task was the election of delegates, not all of whom made their preferences known, the results were inconclusive. Andrea Christianson, then Growe's campaign manager, concluded that Growe was marginally ahead of Anderson and Oberstar with Derus far behind.[10] At about the same time, Bella Abzug was in the Twin Cities to push her new book.[11] In an interview, Abzug fretted that the lack of strong party effort on Growe's behalf reflected a lack of commitment by Minnesota Democrats to the election of women. (It was appropriate that the party be neutral before the state endorsing convention still to come, but Abzug's comment turned out to be more prescient than she might have wished.) The guru of women politicians in the modern era also noted that if women are to succeed, they have to be encouraged to run, to organize early, to be supported by other women with time and money, to have those supporters make noises at caucuses and conventions and to "slam down the lever in the voting booth." Like other women observers of the political scene, Abzug believes that women bring a different dimension to politics — "a certain kind of compassion, a concern for all people, a certain conscientiousness. It's a whole different set of attitudes."[12]

The testing ground for the Growe candidacy came at the state DFL convention which was held at the Civic Center in St. Paul, June 16 and 17. And what a test it turned out to be! The convention's endorsement committee failed to give to any single candidate the requisite 10 votes necessary for recommendation. After three ballots, Growe had eight votes, Oberstar six, Derus and Anderson one each. The committee then agreed to defer the decision to the convention.

Each of the candidates made their pitch to the delegates. Growe emphasized her experience in winning elections, her lead in delegates and fund-raising, and her gain on Boschwitz in the polls.[13] Growe's campaign had also packed the galleries with supporters waving hand-made standards that proclaimed support from every category of citizen — teachers, workers, farmers, nurses and on and on. Those standard-bearers in the galleries were treated to quite a show. When spectators Virginia Greenman, Barbara Stuhler, Mary Vogel-Heffernan, and Jean West talked with each other and with delegate Emily Anne Staples during those two days, little did they know what destiny had in store for them as five members of the still undreamed-of Steering Committee of Minnesota's Groweing.

After the speeches and the demonstrations, the convention went about its business of selecting a candidate for the U.S. Senate. The candidates lobbied the delegates. Anderson, Derus, and Oberstar were hard to spot in their dark suits. Not so Joan Growe who was conspicuous in red and had wisely changed from heels to flats as she moved around the hard cement convention floor. She seemed never to stop, and she was helped by her three older children and by 150 enthusiastic volunteers. The *St. Paul Pioneer Press* reported that "Growe is the front-runner going into today's balloting but no one has the 60 percent needed for endorsement."[14]

The balloting continued throughout the night. After seven ballots, Growe had 48 percent of the vote, Oberstar 39 percent, Derus 8 percent, and Anderson 4 percent. If the convention failed to endorse, there was talk of a primary with even more candidates getting into the act. Among those mentioned were Commissioner of Energy and Development Mark Dayton who had contended unsuccessfully with Independent-Republican David Durenberger for the other Senate seat in 1982, Attorney-General Hubert H. (Skip) Humphrey III, bearer of the name of Minnesota's most beloved political leader, and State Treasurer, Robert Mattson. Mattson, son of a former Attorney-General of Minnesota, had won the 1982 primary over a DFL-endorsed candidate, and his subsequent election was considered something of a political fluke. But it was not the first time that Mattson had confounded the experts or the party.

Finally, on Sunday, June 16, after a 26-hour marathon, Joan Growe was nominated on the 19th ballot.[15] She had received 754 votes, 25 more than the 60 percent required. But the victory did not go unchallenged.

Growe had led on all the ballots starting with the first one at 10:00 A.M. on Saturday, June 16. On Sunday, at 5:30 A.M. — 19½ hours and 14 ballots later — Anderson and Derus released their delegates. At the request of Mary Monohan, DFL Chair, the candidates, their aides, and party officials huddled in a locker room off the convention floor. Out of this discussion there was no agreement except to proceed with the balloting. After the next ballot, there was another huddle and this time the candidates agreed to one more ballot and, if there was no endorsement, so be it. The decision would be made in the primary. But when the 16th ballot produced no endorsement, the convention refused to deal. Anderson withdrew before the 17th ballot. On the 18th ballot, Growe was three votes shy of the magical 60 percent. She went dejectedly to the podium, "I said I would withdraw. I keep my word."[16] Oberstar also bowed out. But the delegates demanded another ballot. As they waited wearily for still another tally, suddenly there were cheers of joy emanating from Growe's workers monitoring the count. Everyone knew then that number 19 would be the final and endorsing ballot — it was 62 percent for Growe. But Joan Growe was a reluctant endorsee. She felt obligated to abide by the terms of the understanding agreed to by the candidates — that the decision would be made in the primary election and not by the convention. She was finally persuaded by Mayor George Latimer of St. Paul, Representative Phyllis Kahn of Minneapolis, and other supporters that it was not her endorsement to refuse or accept—it was the delegates' endorsement, and she really had no choice in the matter. The convention had not been manipulated; it did not consent to any "deal"—the voice of the people (in this case the duly elected DFL delegates) should be heard. Joan Growe went to the platform and accepted her party's endorsement as its candidate for U.S. Senator from Minnesota.[17]

But a nagging question remains. Why was there so little movement to Growe in spite of the fact that she led on every single one of the 19 ballots. Bill Salisbury, respected political columnist of the St. Paul papers, put it down to three factors. Many liberals liked Congressman Jim Oberstar's positions on issues. Even though some disagreed with his pro-life stand, they regarded other issues—the freeze and a generally dovish foreign policy—as more important than abortion. There were others—party veterans and old guard moderates—who were loyal to former Governor Wendy Anderson who had previously been one of the bright lights in the DFL galaxy of promising political leaders. Finally, according to Salisbury, the other candidates were not willing to defer to the front-runner and ask for her endorsement by acclamation.[18] Some did not believe a woman could win in a situation where other viable—and male—candidates were contenders. Many of the Growe supporters—especially the feminists—were convinced that she was denied this customary courtesy as a front-runner because she was a woman.[19]

So Joan Growe won the hard way as she had done before in her contests for the legislative seat and for the position of Secretary of State. There were a lot of bruised feelings. Supporters of the other candidates felt that Growe had not kept her word as the balloting proceeded beyond the negotiated deadline. But she had no more command over that convention than did the other contenders. She was persistent, yes, and she held her supporters throughout the long ordeal. The Growe campaign had been well-organized and managed primarily, if not exclusively, by women. It was another sign that women were coming of political age.[20]

The other candidates hinted that they might enter the primary. And these rumors persisted until Anderson, Derus, and Oberstar withdrew. Derus had taken himself out of the race immediately. Anderson was the last to step aside on July 5. He was, according to reports, swayed by the advice of politically active friends who said that he would divide the party beyond hope of repair in time for the November 6 general election.[21] Earlier, D. J. Leary, an astute observer of Minnesota politics, had stated, "Wendy would bring strong negatives into the campaign. He has a history of being badly served by his personal ambition."[22] Robert Mattson, however, did enter the primary as he promised to do if Growe received the endorsement. When he filed on July 3, he stated that his mainstream candidacy offered voters an alternative to the liberalism of Growe and the conservatism of Boschwitz.[23]

Even though Mattson had not been a contender for convention endorsement, DFLers and other Growe supporters were worried. Mattson had taken on party-endorsed candidates four times and had won twice.[24] When he was elected Treasurer in 1982, he had sat out most of the campaign in Florida, coasting on the name recognition he inherited from his father who had been Minnesota's Attorney General from 1964 to 1966.[25] An editorial in the *St. Paul Pioneer Press* posed the issue:

> "A *few observations on the primary system in Minnesota: (1) the election will be only two months before the general election, hardly sufficient time for the winner to campaign effectively; (2) it will be an open primary — as open to Independent-Republicans as DFLers. The second factor will make it very difficult to determine the meaning of the outcome of the primary;*

*the first will make it difficult for voters to assess their
choices in November."*[26]

Growe filed three days after Mattson on July 6, 1984.
There were many who were leery of the Growe-Mattson
primary contest. Mattson had defeated DFL-endorsed candidates two times before, but that was not the only concern.
Other favored DFL candidates had gone down to defeat in
Minnesota primary elections. In 1966 when the DFL party
endorsed Lieutenant Governor A. M. (Sandy) Keith over incumbent Governor Karl F. Rolvaag, the voters chose Rolvaag over Keith by nearly 180,000 votes in the primary election. In the 1978 senatorial primary, the DFL-endorsed
candidate, Congressman Donald Fraser (currently mayor
of Minneapolis), lost to challenger Robert Short by a vote of
257,269 to 253,818. Because Minnesota has an open primary, there is some suspicion that upsets such as these may
have been generated in some measure by Republican voters
who "crossed over" to make sure that the DFL candidate
most likely to lose to the Republican candidate would win
in the primary. In both these instances, the Republican candidate did go on to win the general election. That suspicion
or apprehension was a critical determinant in the organization of Minnesota's Groweing.[27]

In her first press conference as a formal candidate,
Growe chose the Minneapolis Federal Reserve Bank as a
backdrop for her assertion that the economy — especially
high interest rates — would be a prime issue in the general
election.[28] Although concerned with the primary contest,
Growe continued to look past Mattson in her campaign
rhetoric and prepare for the ultimate contest with Rudy
Boschwitz.[29]

In the aftermath of the state convention, another memor-
able event occured. Walter F. Mondale, the apparent
presidential nominee of the Democratic party, chose
Representative Geraldine Ferraro of New York to be his
running mate. It was almost too much. A man from Min-

nesota would head the first major party ticket with a woman as the vice presidential candidate. A woman from Minnesota would be the first in the state to be the choice of one of the two major parties for the U.S. Senate.[30] Minnesota feminists were beside themselves with joy.

Growe went to the Democratic National Convention seeking to establish a national image for herself. Thanks to being from the same state as the presidential nominee, she was given a slot on the convention program, speaking on agricultural policies. It was mid-afternoon, however, and less than prime time but delegates saw and heard her. She made the round of parties, an important vehicle for making yourself and your candidacy known to potential contributors. She also was one of the principal subjects of a "Frontline" national television program. "Be careful what you say to me," she warned friends, "I'm wired for sound."[31] Then it was back to Minnesota and the campaign.

While Growe was trying to downplay the Mattson candidacy, there were other rumblings on the horizon. A national poll, reported in the *St. Paul Pioneer Press* on July 1, indicated that a woman on the national Democratic ticket would make no difference to the vast majority of voters. Eleven percent said that they would be more likely to vote for the Democrats but 16 percent said they would then be less likely to vote for the Democratic ticket.[32] Furthermore, Republican strategists in Minnesota claimed that Growe was not the strongest contender. In their view, Oberstar who would appeal to both rural conservatives (because of his opposition to the pro-choice position) and urban liberals (foreign policy issues in particular), would be the hardest to beat. Growe could exploit the gender gap and capture the freeze vote but would lose conservatives who wouldn't cast their ballots for a woman.[33] No one gave much thought to the possibility of Growe bringing a new constituency — women — to the polls on primary election day. Except for occasional close contests, voters in Minnesota do not go the polls in great numbers in primary elections because the party endorsement system usually determines who the candidates will be.[34]

As the Growe campaign moved from caucus to convention to primary, it began to change. An experienced state Senator, Steven Novak of New Brighton, became the campaign manager.[35] It became big-time and necessarily so, even though the successful 1982 Perpich-Johnson campaign had been waged with very little money or media. But the need for money was very real if only because the Republican incumbent had so much of it. Growe supporters were inundated with invitations to benefits. Much of that money would be spent on the media. There were jobs to be done in campaign headquarters — essential tasks of scheduling, preparing materials, planning debates, briefing and informing the candidate on a whole host of national issues. But there were a lot of people out there — mostly women — who could afford only so many benefits and whose time or interests simply did not coincide with the requirements of a campaign headquarters or its outposts in Greater Minnesota. There was also some suspicion that DFL party leaders were not entirely united around the Growe candidacy. Something had to be done to provide women with an opportunity to bridge the gap between money-givers and party-workers and to infuse the campaign with enthusiasm and elan. Something had to be done to enlist the energies of the many Growe Supporters — women in particular — who wanted to be part of the effort to put Joan Growe into the United States Senate. Minnesota's Groweing would provide an opportunity for that participation.

2 | The Cast of Characters

THE PRODUCERS AND DIRECTORS of the Minnesota's Groweing campaign were the members of the Steering Committee. These ten women — some of whom conceived the idea and the imagery — shared a common interest in politics, a commitment to feminism, and a belief that there is still a role for grass-roots involvement in campaigns even as big as one involving a candidate for the United States Senate. These were the 10 who began the pyramid, who brought a variety of experiences and talents to the organization, and who achieved a notable success in getting out the vote for Joan Growe in the primary election on September 11, 1984.

* * *

VIRGINIA G. GREENMAN is a consultant in innovative health design. Until the late 1960s, she had been an active Republican and a member of the Ripon Society. But she switched parties because she found her pro-choice preference incompatible with the mainstream Minnesota GOP. After returning to college and obtaining a B. A. in political science from the University of Minnesota in 1970, she went to work for the Bipartisan Caucus to End the War in Viet-

nam. In 1972, she ran for the Ramsey County Board of
Commissioners and came in fourth — though the top woman
— in a primary field of 18. Her appointment by Mayor
Larry Cohen as chair of the first St. Paul cable television
task force was followed by two subsequent appointments by
Governor Wendell Anderson to the state board on cable television. Greenman once again became a student, this time
earning a master's degree in public health from the University of Minnesota, her interest prompted by her involvement with InterStudy, a nationally recognized think tank
on health care issues. Greenman's political interests were inspired by her mother — a daughter of Norwegian immi-
grants — who voted in the 1920 election, some three months
after the passage of the 19th amendment. Ruth Gregg never
forgot that experience nor the reason why her parents
emigrated: to enjoy the benefits of a free and democratic society and to contribute to the well-being of that society.
That message and the admonition that "it is a sin not to
vote" were legacies to her daughter. Ginny Greenman, who
has always been driven by a desire to change things for the
better, was a wise and energetic member of the Steering
Committee of Minnesota's Groweing.

LINDA L. HOLSTEIN practices law in Minneapolis,
specializing in the area of commercial litigation. Linda
came by her political interests naturally. Her parents,
Arthur and "Pete" Holstein of Tracy, Minnesota, are lifelong
Democrats. Holstein's first political memory is her mother
sobbing over the loss of Adlai E. Stevenson to Dwight D.
Eisenhower in the 1952 presidential election. In the Holstein household, Franklin D. Roosevelt was a "saint," John
F. Kennedy "walked with the gods," and Hubert H. Humphrey deserved "canonization." Before entering law school
at the University of Minnesota, Holstein taught theatre,
speech, and English for 10 years, primarily in the Robbinsdale school district. She has been a member of the state
Democratic-Farmer-Labor Central Committee and a two-

time delegate to the state convention. In 1960, she helped manage Emily Anne Staples' reelection campaign for the Minnesota Senate. Linda Holstein was the live wire of Minnesota's Groweing, anticipating victory, fretting over details, and serving as speaker "par excellence."

RUBY HUNT is a member of the Board of Ramsey County Commissioners from District 5. She was elected to that position in 1982 after serving for 10 years on the St. Paul City Council. Born and reared in St. Paul, her interest in state politics developed at the time she served as the PTA lobbyist at the Legislature, and her involvement in local politics was stimulated by her membership in and subsequent presidency of the St. Paul League of Women Voters. Hunt's main interest in government has been in its structure — a basic and vital consideration, however prosaic it may seem to the voters. But Hunt has never lost an election! She was moved to seek office on the city council by her experience as Chair of the St. Paul Charter Commission in 1972. Once that new charter had been approved by the voters (and Hunt played a key role in securing that approval), she wanted to be part of the implementation through the development of the administrative code. Her decision, a decade later, not to seek reelection was prompted by a sense that she had accomplished her major goal with the establishment of a new and strong mayor/council form of government for her city. Her decision to run for the Ramsey County Commission was stimulated by a similar concern — that cronyism in county government should be replaced by professionalism. She is still working at that task. Ruby Hunt brought to the Minnesota's Groweing Steering Committee important dimensions both of enthusiasm and of experience as an elected public official.

MYRNA MAROFSKY is President of Computer Encounter, a division of Kid's Network which trains adults and children to use micro-computers. She is a graduate of the University of Minnesota's College of Education and has worked as a professional educator, author, and trainer for over 15 years. Currently, she serves on the Governor's Commission on Technology in Education and as a member of the Board of Advisers of the Employer Education Service, a unit of the Industrial Relations Center in the University's School of Management. Marofsky has been active in DFL politics as a delegate to state and local conventions and as a senate district coordinator for several candidates. She managed the campaigns for former Senator Emily Anne Staples in 1976 and 1980. When she ran for the Board of Robbinsdale School District #281 (where she had previously taught) in 1980, she lost by nine votes. There was a recount resulting in a tie that was decided against her by a toss of a coin. But she won in 1981, losing again in 1984 when her supporters — thinking her well-organized and a certain victor — failed to go to the polls. Like other members of the Steering Committee, she was greatly influenced by her family, most particularly by her first generation Russian immigrant father, a man who transmitted his commitment to liberal ideas and ideals to his daughter. Myrna Marofsky, as Treasurer of Minnesota's Groweing, was a key figure bringing experience and know-how to the organization and a thoughtfulness that informed us all.

MARTHA H. NORTON is a life-time resident of St. Paul and a long-time political activist. She first became interested in politics as a young woman because of her father's involvement in the civic affairs of that city. In the early 1960s, she was coordinator of women's activities for the state DFL party organization. In that period she worked on the campaigns of several prominent legislators and chaired the women's committee for the last senatorial campaign of Eugene J. McCarthy. In 1966, she became one of the highest ranking women in the party, serving for the next six years as Vice Chairwoman and issues coordinator, organizing task forces on such critical issues as pollution, nuclear power, metropolitan government, transportation, and taxes. In the 1970s, she was a member and subsequently became chair of the St. Paul Planning Commission. In 1980-81, she worked in Washington, D. C. for the Department of Energy. She continues to be involved in the politics of her community, state, and nation. It was no surprise that Martie Norton was the convenor of the group that ultimately became Minnesota's Groweing.

KATHLEEN KENNEDY SCOTT was born in New York, grew up in Minneapolis, and returned to her native state for her college education, receiving a Bachelor's degree from Manhattanville College. After graduate study at the University of Minnesota and a brief career as a social worker in Catholic Charities, she settled into life as a homemaker and volunteer. Some of her activities included service as a director of the Minnesota Orchestral Association and as president of the Young People's Symphony Orchestra. More recently, she has been a founding director of the Minnesota Women's Campaign Fund and a volunteer with the Dorothy Day Center in St. Paul. She is also vitally concerned with the preservation of our natural environment, serving as a trustee of Nature Conservancy, and being instrumental in the establishment of Minnesota's North Shore Peregrine Falcon project. An influential aunt sparked her original interest in politics, but Scott's active involvement was precipitated by her antipathy to war. Her brother was killed training bomber pilots for the Korean War, and she became an early supporter of Eugene McCarthy as he articulated the growing American sentiment against the war in Vietnam. Although Scott says that her commitment to feminism has been more individual than organizational, she takes pride in the fact that "my daughters learned feminist guerilla tactics at my knee." Kathleen Scott approached every task with energy and good humor.

EMILY ANNE STAPLES is Director of Community Relations for Spring Hill Center, a widely-used conference facility located west of Minneapolis. A state senator from 1977-81, she was the first of her party and the third woman in Minnesota to be elected to that office. A life-long political activist, she was a Republican until 1973 when she switched her affiliation to the Democratic-Farmer-Labor party after the Minnesota GOP refused to support the Equal Rights Amendment. After her defeat for re-election in a contest that still stands as the most expensive ever waged for a Minnesota senate seat, Staples received a Bush Foundation grant to attend the John F. Kennedy School of Government at Harvard University where she received a Master of Public Administration degree in 1982. Staples' first political experience was at age three when her father – an attorney and newspaper man – took her to see Franklin D. Roosevelt. Her mother, by her example as a teacher and volunteer, instilled in her a sense of public service. Over the years, Staples has held national positions with the Junior League, the Overseas Education Fund, the United Way, the Interstate Association of Commissions on the Status of Women, and the National Trust for Historic Preservation. In Minnesota, she has been active in and an officer of a variety of civic, educational, and cultural organizations. Emily Anne Staples is a respected leader in the community – "ubiquitous," some have said – and her presence in Minnesota's Groweing brought prestige and public relations skills to the organization.

BARBARA STUHLER is Associate Dean of Continuing Education and Extension (CEE) at the University of Minnesota. Before her appointment to that position, she was Associate Director of the World Affairs Center, then affiliated with the University as a department of CEE. In the 1950s and 1960s, she was active in the League of Women Voters, serving as vice president of the Minnesota League and as foreign policy chair for four of her six years on the national League's board of directors. Her experience at the University and with the League coalesced into a concern for the opportunities of women in positions of administrative and political leadership. That concern was reinforced by the experience of co-editing — with Gretchen Kreuter — *Women of Minnesota: Selected Biographical Essays* published by the Minnesota Historical Society in 1977. More recently, Stuhler has served as president of CHART, a career development organization for women, and was co-chair — with Martha Atwater — of the Minnesota Women's Campaign Fund from 1984 to 1986. Her long-time interest in politics began when she was in college, a rebel of sorts against her family's conservative Republicanism. Barbara Stuhler wrote most of the Minnesota's Groweing materials, counted money and signatures, and served as co-host with Jean West of the many meetings of the Steering Committee that took place at their residence in St. Paul.

MARY VOGEL-HEFFERNAN is coordinator of research in the School of Architecture at the University of Minnesota. Prior to her appointment to that position in November 1985 and during the period of the Minnesota's Groweing campaign, she was with the St. Paul architectural firm, Val Michaelson and Associates. Vogel-Heffernan, a native of Red Wing, Minnesota, was part of a politically active family and remembers first campaigning at the age of 10. In her adult years, she changed her party allegiance and served on the staff for the senatorial campaign of Eugene McCarthy in 1967-68. From 1968-70, she was Ramsey County chairwoman and on the executive committee of the DFL party. She was one of a group of women, including Virginia Greenman — then a Republican — who founded the Ramsey Women's Political Caucus in 1971. Her concern with women's issues in combination with her profession led to the first design — in collaboration with a professor at the University's School of Architecture — of a battered women's shelter. She is president of the Minnnesota Association of Women in Housing and in 1984 was a convenor of the first national workshop on housing as a woman's issue in

Washington, D. C. Her participation as a member of the Steering Committee of Minnesota's Groweing was a natural outcome of her long-time commitment to the women's movement, to the DFL party, and to her small-town upbringing — she believed in the grass roots. The name, Minnesota's Groweing, was Mary Vogel-Heffernan's idea.

JEAN M.WEST is president of two companies, Carleton J. West Publications and West Premium Corporation. She is also a member of the Committee of 200, a prestigious organization of women business leaders. A life-long resident of St. Paul, she takes great pride in her city and has served on a vast array of community boards. She attributes her volunteer involvement to her early training as a member of the Junior League. Some of her recent presidencies include Chimera Theatre, Neighborhood House, and COMPAS. Currently, she is a commissioner of the St. Paul Port Authority, a director of the Northwest Area Foundation, and a founding board member of the Minnesota Women's Campaign Fund. She chaired the first two years of the YWCA leadership award program for outstanding women in St. Paul and in 1982 was recognized for achievement in volunteer service. It was West who initiated the idea of a pyramid organization for Minnesota's Groweing. Her business acumen was essential to its efficient operation. She knew suppliers, negotiated space for assembling materials, and was an eternal optimist about the outcome. Jean West, who changed from a Republican to a Democrat in the 1964 Johnson-Goldwater presidential contest, infuses politics with the same verve and enthusiasm that characterizes her other interests and activities.

*   *   *

If these ten women served as the producers and directors, the stars of Minnesota's Groweing were all those thousands of women and some men who signed up voters for Growe.

3 The Beginning

IN A WAY IT ALL BEGAN with Martie Norton — or at least she served as the catalyst to bring together the women who became the nucleus of Minnesota's Groweing. Norton had previously been deeply involved in Democratic-Farmer-Labor politics. She was a friend of Joan Growe and, although more recently she had set her sights on activities other than politics, she could not resist the temptation of involvement with Growe's bid for the U.S. Senate. Norton's predilection was similar to that of other women poised on the fringe of the Growe campaign.

Growe had asked Norton to serve on her finance committee but Norton did not like fund-raising and said so. Norton was also upset over the general direction of Growe's campaign which seemed to some to put a greater premium on image rather than organization. To Norton, the key ingredients were organization and outreach. She felt strongly that the missing link in the Growe campaign, following her endorsement by the DFL state convention, was the lack of opportunity for women to participate in a meaningful way. The choices were either raising money (and some women did that) or campaign scut-work — the necessary but routine chores which in earlier years had been characteristic of women's work in politics. In 1984, most women were too busy at other tasks. If they were going to contribute their time and energy, it had to be at a more significant level of activity. There was also a sense that the Growe campaign was now being run in traditional ways by traditional (and male) political pros. There seemed to be very little in the way of direction or strategy—the concentration was on money, not organization. Suggestions by Norton and others of the need to establish networks, to reach out to women, and to do those things that would distinguish a woman's campaign for the United States Senate fell on deaf ears.[1]

Norton, talking with others—Virginia Greenman, Jan Hively, Yvette Oldendorf, and Mary Vogel-Heffernan— found them of like mind. Some of them got together for lunch to discuss various ideas to generate support for Joan Growe. There needed to be, they agreed, a groundswell for their candidate, but there was nothing in sight producing it. The effort that had generated Growe delegates—and ultimately won the endorsement—out of the precinct caucuses, state senatorial, and district conventions was apparently dissipated as more established figures took command and determined that the resources of the campaign would be diverted from grass-roots organizing to other purposes.[2]

At about this same time—on June 27—the Minnesota Women's Campaign Fund held its annual fund-raising reception. Campaign Fund Guarantors (women who pledge $1,000 to the organization over a two-year period) were invited to a pre-reception seminar with women incumbents and candidates. Arvonne Fraser, a Campaign Fund Board member, led the discussion. Norton was there. The women present were both informed and moved by the experience.[3]

Norton, especially impressed with Myrna Marofsky who had recently lost a school board race in Robbinsdale, spoke with her and also with Arvonne Fraser about the Growe campaign. They, too, shared Norton's views.

Following the reception, a dozen or so Campaign Fund

board members had dinner at the Nicollet Island Inn. They rehashed the event and talked especially about Joan Growe's campaign – she had been there and spoke briefly. The group had a vested interest in Growe – early on the Fund had given her $5,000 (and after the primary election would give her $5,000 more). Though they were Independents and Republicans as well as Democrats, they shared the excitement evoked by a woman's candidacy for high public office.

The conversation began to focus on several questions. Was Growe going to wage a traditional man's political campaign? Was she going to spend all her resources on the media? What about the grass roots? What about the role of women in this campaign? Of course, those on the outside often think they can do whatever it is "better," but these were serious and valid questions. Later, Arvonne Fraser, one of the diners that night and an experienced DFL campaigner, would attempt to speak to some of the Growe staff about these concerns. She was not well-received. The campaign manager was late for the appointment and then seemed distracted and disinterested in Fraser's ideas.[4]

One thing was clear. There were a lot of politically interested women who were willing to commit themselves to a women's effort in the Growe campaign, but they were frustrated because no one in charge seemed willing to act upon their suggestions. It was their perception that there was little interest in a commitment to running a woman's campaign differently. Growe's convention endorsement was the product of grass-roots organizing done in large part by women. Although Growe herself never rejected women as a resource – witness the number in key campaign posts – nevertheless, the campaign drifted to the center and to what many women political activists perceived as the traditional "male" way of doing such things.

Some time later, Norton encountered Emily Anne Staples who was equally distressed over the course of events. In a subsequent phone conversation, Staples suggested that Norton invite some of these concerned women to her summer house on the St. Croix River for further discussion that coming Saturday—July 14. Staples would ask Marofsky (who had served as her campaign manager) to come. Norton called Fraser who was away at the Democratic National Convention in San Francisco. Greenman was out of town. Mary Vogel-Heffernan would be there. Remembering the stimulating discussion that had evolved at the Campaign Fund's seminar, Norton called Barbara Stuhler and asked if she and Jean West could come. They would. Although some of us might have been enticed by the idea of spending a summer Saturday on the St. Croix, it rained all day. It was just as well—we were not distracted by the prospects of a swim or boat-ride.

Only Norton and Staples knew the cast of characters in their entirety. We were six in all and although some knew each other well, others were strangers—but not for long. Stuhler recalled the day:

"We got down to business almost immediately. It was a good group, but I had no idea then how intimately we were going to be involved over the next four months. We were after ideas, and a lot of them spewed forth. West introduced the concept of the pyramid by telling of a book (and she still can't remember which one it was) in which an expanding group was organized by long-distance phone calls to elect someone to office. Marofsky had had some experience with building such a pyramid in her own school board campaign. We went on to other ideas. We were especially taken with the notion of involving all of Greater Minnesota (a relatively new term describing those parts of the state outside the Twin Cities metropolitan area). We were excited about the prospect of reaching out to every county. We speculated about county fairs, about a local contact in every county, a newspaper ad in all the local papers featuring Growe and a distinguished citi-

zen of the community. But it was already too late.
County fairs were underway, and the organizational
problems seemed unsurmountable."

Marofsky returned to the pyramid idea, and we soon discussed it in earnest. It had an appealing simplicity. Ten women would be responsible for getting 10 women (100) who would recruit another 10 (1,000) who would enlist another 10 (10,000) who would then sign up 10 men and women as voters for Growe (100,000). We even went as high as one million in our initial calculations but soon decided that was an unrealistic expectation. Its appeal was that no one would be responsible for more than 10 — it was manageable. Further, it provided women with an opportunity to make a contribution to Growe's candidacy — grassroots women who otherwise might not be involved.

Vogel-Heffernan had come up with the name, "Minnesota's Groweing," and Staples suggested buttons. West refined the idea, "Button are buttons. Let's number the buttons from 1 to 100,000." We made two more decisions — to add four to our numbers to make the starting 10 and to have the 10 meet for breakfast at the Minneapolis Club four days later on Wednesday, July 18.

As we left Martie Norton's that rainy Saturday afternoon, none of us knew then the extent of the effort before us. We had a concept — the pyramid. We had a name — Minnesota's Groweing. We had a graphic gimmick — a numbered button. And we had a commitment — to turn a big primary win for Joan Growe into a prologue for her ultimate victory in the race for the United State Senate. It was a start.

4 | The Organization

FOUR DAYS AFTER the Norton "summit" meeting on the St. Croix, 10 women arrived for breakfast at the Minneapolis Club. There was a certain symbolism in the suggestion by Emily Anne Staples of our next meeting place — it was, after all, not until 1977 that women could enter the front door of the Minneapolis Club.[1] In those earlier times, women entered by the back door and came for social reasons. Now, women also meet there to do business. We were there to attend to the business of politics. Linda Holstein remembers Staples' phone call:

> " 'Linda, can you come to breakfast at the Minneapolis Club on Wednesday? At 7:30 A.M.? For Joan Growe? These marvelous women I know are forming an independent committee — we're not quite sure about our actual plans. But Jean West has this fascinating idea.'
> . . .It is hard to say no to Emily Anne. When she called my office and told me about a breakfast for 10 women, I did not hesitate. Yes, I would be there. It was not often that I had the chance to start my day at the Minneapolis Club, even if was at the ungodly hour of 7:30 A.M. I presumed I might have to contribute a

29

*hundred dollars or so but at least I would get a decent
plate of eggs and be at the office in good time. As political commitments go, this one sounded simple. One
thing I knew for sure. I was not going to get tangled
up in some fundraising scheme where I had to peddle
a cause over the phone. Just write the check and get
out of there — that was my plan."*

Little did Holstein then know that money was not the immediate object nor that she would not "get out of there"
without a very large commitment to a new dimension of the
Growe campaign.

After the initial pyramid plan was devised on that rainy
Saturday at Martie Norton's St.Croix River house, we were
faced with trying to translate 10 to the fifth power from
numbers to people. How would the Committee of 10 ever
know what was going on with the Committee of 10,000.
The answer was easy; we wouldn't. But we had to know
how the 10, 100, 1,000 and 10,000 would function in order
to prepare instructions and to order materials in appropriate quantities.

During that first meeting — on Wednesday, July 18 — of
what would become the Committee of 10 (and later the
Steering Committee), the mechanics of "a system" had been
developed. Even the skeptics were convinced that it could
work. The 10 of us would get 10 women who would get 10
women who would get 10 men and women to get 10 voters
to sign up for Growe. Simple. All the way up or down the
pyramid, no one had to contact more than 10.

We would name each level accordingly. We were the
Committee of 10 who would find 10 women to constitute
the Committee of 100. Each of the 100 would find 10
women and they would become the Committee of 1,000.
The 10, 100, and 1,000 would come to a breakfast early in
August, and that breakfast would serve as the kickoff of
Minnesota's Groweing. More importantly, it would serve as
the easiest method of distributing all the materials through-

out the pyramid. At the kickoff, the Committee of 1,000 would be instructed to increase the pyramid one more level by getting 10 men and women who would become the Committee of 10,000. The materials (still to be devised) would then be made available so that everybody from the 10 to the 10,000 would have a campaign kit and instructions as to how to continue the pyramid. Wonderful! The Committee of 10,000 would sign up 10 voters each for Growe (and so would the 10, 100, and 1,000). We would go into the primary with 100,000 votes (our goal) and with any luck, a bit to spare. It was so simple, it was complicated. But the Committee of 10 on July 18 feigned total comprehension, and the pyramid was a "go" before we had finished our breakfast. Minnesota's Groweing would be an independent political committee and, in less than eight weeks, would sign up 100,000 plus voters for Joan Growe through a grass-roots, low-cost, people-intensive effort.

Linda Holstein as usual – or soon we were to discover – was late. She has characterized the event in her own inimitable style:

"There were nine women seated around a long table in one of the second floor meeting rooms. I scrutinized the faces around the table and recognized Myrna Marofsky. She was describing how a telephone pyramid had worked in Plymouth for a Robbinsdale School Board race. Then Staples introduced Jean West whom I'd never met. As West starting talking, I realized that this wasn't a plea for money after all. I remember thinking '10 women. That's the sum total of what I really have to do. Find 10 women and my responsibility is over.' West rhapsodized about 'a pyramid of 100,000 women.' One hundred thousand? This woman was obviously a political neophyte. She kept saying, '10 get 100 get 1,000 get 10,000.' But I kept saying to myself, 'Holstein, you only need to find 10 believers and let the rest of these optimists worry

*about the masses.' My naivete lasted approximately
five minutes. All of us, it was clear, would take care of
the masses. According to West, we could only keep
track of them by using individual button numbers.
People in Ely and Pipestone and Caledonia would buy
a button because, she said, the would have their very
own number on it. I pictured the person who bought
button number 45,000 placing an ad in the Twin Cities Reader: 'Political Junkie seeks soulmate wearing
Minnesota's Groweing Button No. 45,00l.' But West
was serious. She already had two alternative dates for
a kickoff breakfast at the Prom Center in St. Paul. Barbara Stuhler explained why the event had to start at
7:30 A.M. also, since working women had a limited
amount of time on weekdays. Fine, I thought, but
couldn't we find some bar where 1,000 women might
like to have an evening cocktail after work? They ignored me. I knew then that I had signed on with some
classic 'morning-is-better' types."*[2]

Anticipating approval of the pyramid plan, West had
mapped out a calendar of what needed to be done from July
18 to the September 11 primary, and the Prom Center had
been asked to put a temporary hold on all available dates
they had open the first and second weeks in August for a
kickoff breakfast. The Prom Center, which was in the Midway district (not downtown Minneapolis and not downtown St. Paul but large enough to accommdodate us in an
inbetween location), would hold those dates until 11:00
A.M. that very morning. The Committee of 10, who at that
point had not been given any time to question whether or
not they intended to be part of the Committe of 10, suddenly found that a very crucial date decision had to be
made immediately. We selected August 9 which would give
us three weeks to get all the materials (whatever they might
be) printed and assembled and then there would be four
and a-half weeks after the kickoff to complete the last level

of the pyramid and sign up the voters. That August 9 date was a gutsy decision especially because we had no idea of how long it would take to prepare any materials and to assemble same.

It was getting late that morning and several had to get to jobs or other meetings. Calendars came out of purses to decide when we should meet again. Forget it. We had to meet again immediately. We were already out of time for what we had to do. We asked what everyone was doing for lunch (too many conflicts) and set the next meeting for that same night at Mary Vogel-Heffernan's house. In the meantime some assignments had been agreed to. Vogel-Heffernan was in charge of designing the button, Marofsky would be treasurer and arrange all of the details of setting up our committee with the State Ethical Practices Board, and West would get the estimates of button prices.

West recalled the button drama (trauma?):

"It was the beginning of an unbelievable day. We needed 150,000 buttons, numbered in sequence, delivered as soon as possible and in less than three weeks. I called eight local suppliers of buttons. The best any of them could do was 5,000 per week with two weeks lead time. The buttons were essential. They were to be our product, our income and, with each one numbered, our gimmick. I started calling around the country after getting names of companies from the St. Paul Public Library. I reached button machine manufacturers, a button works that made brass buttons for the military, and an eastern manufacturer who was much too quick to promise he could meet our deadline with an air freight delivery on the final day. By afternoon I was frantic. I would have to go to the 7:30 P.M. meeting and cancel the project for lack of a product. Somehow, after a Sherlock Holmes adventure in trying to find a button manufacturer by begging for one referral after another, I found LarLu Line in Winona,

*Minnesota. I couldn't believe it. After Chicago, Mil-
waukee, New Jersey and Texas—right in Minnesota,
100 miles away. Yes, it would be difficult but LarLu
thought it could deliver. If we contracted directly with
Winona Printing to print the face of the button, and
if Winona Printing could get the printed sheets to
LarLu by the following Tuesday, all delivery commitments would be contingent on the ability to begin cap-
ping the buttons no later than the early morning of
July 25 (that was a week hence!) I called Winona
Printing to describe the two-color buttons (which had
not as yet been designed) numbered from 1 to 150,000.
The printer called LarLu. I called LarLu. LarLu
called the printer. The printer called me and, by 5:30
P.M., I had the home number for Steve Styba at
LarLu and the names of four men at Winona Printing,
one or all of whom would do their best to let me know
the next day whether or not they could handle our
order."*

The meeting at Mary Vogel-Heffernan's was one of instant decision-making. Mary had a button design underway, with "Minnesota's Groweing" in white letters on a
green field, and the numbering would be in reflex blue, and
we all approved. Yes, we should forget about trying to get
competitive bids for buttons—we were lucky to have one
pending! Yes, the Prom Center had been called at 11:00
A.M. that morning, and the August 9 date for the kickoff
was confirmed. Yes, several of the Committee of 10 had already started calling their 10, and thus the Committee of
100 was underway.

At the breakfast in the Minneapolis club on July 18,
Marie Weiss (an executive with General Mills and a friend
and political compatriot of Marofsky and Staples) had
pulled out her checkbook to write a check for startup costs.
We quickly decided that no one would put up any money.
We would get a bank loan for our supplies as soon as we

could get a preliminary budget worked out — and Barbara Stuhler could sign the note! Right after breakfast, West called Gary Woelke at First Bank St. Paul, told him what we thought we were doing and that we would like to borrow $20,000 for 60 days on Stuhler's signature. What was the rate and what did we need to do? Woelke sent a financial statement that afternoon for Stuhler to fill out and said that the account would be set up on whatever day we wanted the loan to take effect. So, in the 12 hours from the first meeting of the Committee of 10 to the meeting at Vogel-Heffernan's, we had the time schedule, money in the bank, we were registered as a political committee and, depending upon an okay from Winona Printing the next day, we would have our 150,000 buttons.

Thursday, July 19 was a beautiful summer day — most of the days from July 18 to August 9 were beautiful — but there was little time to notice. West recalled:

"I remember that particular day as beautiful for a good reason. I had called Bill Lang at Winona Printing, and he had said that the only way they could get the sheets of buttons printed to meet the LarLu deadline would be if they could have the button design, camera-ready, before the end of the day. Otherwise there were no promises. I called Vogel-Heffernan envisioning that she could get the necessary artwork finished in the morning, and then I would get in my car to race a piece of paper 100 miles to Winona. I knew it was a beautiful day because Vogel-Heffernan knew it was a beautiful day, and she was on a boat on the St Croix River 20 miles away and unable to be reached. Where was the button design? I called one of Mary's sons every hour. Was she home? Had she called home? Was he sure she wouldn't be back until after 6:00 P.M.? Did he leave a message by every phone asking her to call me immediately?

"At least I had plenty of time to figure out some way

to get the button artwork to Winona without having to drive it there myself. There are always buses. And buses take packages. I talked again with Bill Lang at Winona Printing and explained that I couldn't get the art work to him until the next day. Please — could they still make the LarLu deadline? By this time Bill, who had no idea who this persistent woman was calling him every 10 minutes, certainly knew I was serious about placing this order with him. He agreed that he would start setting up time on his presses. Furthermore, he would meet the 5:35 P.M. bus the next day and work over the weekend to get the order started. I hoped that Vogel-Heffernan had had a restful, beautiful day on the river because Friday morning it would take all her energy to transform her sketch of the button design into final keyline, camera-ready art and get it packaged for its bus ride on the 12:10 P.M. to Winona.

"On Friday, early in the afternoon, I called Bill to tell him that the package was on the bus. Mary was a heroine, indeed."

The Committe of 10 met again on Saturday, and West had agreed to get cost estimates for other materials. She continued:

"Jerry McCarthy, owner of Chase Printing Company, reponded to my pleading for instant bids. I was vague on quantities and vague on what we needed printed. Did we want two-part or three-part signature sheets? With carbons or carbonless? Did we want 10,000 letters printed on one side or two? What did we need?

"We had not had time as a group to go step by step through the pyramid process to determine what we needed. Unfortunately, we would never have the luxury of that kind of time. Someone had to figure it all out and not wait for approval on each tiny detail before proceeding. There was no time for a second or

*third bid on printing unknown materials in unknown
quantities. We knew we needed a descriptive piece on
Joan Growe, an instruction sheet, a signature sheet, a
time schedule, buttons, some kind of kit to put everything in, and some kind of container to hold 10 kits
each. Grabbing a piece of paper, I calculated the
quantity. We need 10,000 kits. No, we need 10,000 +
1,000 + 100 + 10. A manila envelope would be large
enough to hold a few sheets of paper and ten buttons.
No way could we find 10,000 manila envelopes without finding a wholesaler. I asked McCarthy if he could
get them for us. Whoops! We don't need 10,000 we
need 11,110. Jerry suggested we could save printing instruction sheets by printing that information on the
manila envelopes. Marvelous. I would take that suggestion to the Committee. So please give us a quote on
10,000 — no, 11,110 envelopes blank and 11,110 envelopes printed on one side. And we need 100,000 Joan
Growe information sheets — no, 111,110. And we need
a bid on 111,110 signature sheets — no, at two for each
kit, it would be 222,200. Well, bid on carbonless two-
part and three-part. No, we don't need white envelopes, manila is fine. Of course, the Committee may
not approve . . . or we may decide on different
quantities. McCarthy called back with the price quo-
tations by noon on Friday and made it to his golf game
after all, but not without asking if he could have the
copy by Monday?"*

Meanwhile, meeting number three of the full Committee
of 10 had been set. We would meet on Saturday, July 21 at
Emily Anne Staples'. It was fortuitous choice. Unlike the
previous rainy Saturday when the original six met at Norton's, this day was hot and humid. So Staples' pool proved
to be a life-saver as we intermittently planned on land and
plunged in water. In either case, as Linda Holstein observed, "We were making waves."

July and August are not the best times of the year for organizing a late-coming campaign like Minnesota's Groweing. Families and vacations put other demands on the 10 so not everyone was present at every meeting. Even so,the attendance was better than average throughout this frantic period. On this day we were six and our chores were several. We hoped to prepare the necessary materials. We needed to define the kinds of women who should constitute the Committee of 100 and come up with a sales pitch they could not resist. We had to review where we were, what progress we had made, and make sure we had not forgotten anything in the process. It was a tall order, and we spent six hours of intense discussion at the task.

There was a newcomer in the cast of characters. Earlier that morning, West had called Staples and asked if she could bring Ruby Hunt, whom she had already signed on as a member of the Committee of 100. That was fine with Staples who took pains to point out, "Jean, you know Democrats are inclusive, not exclusive." Hunt's enthusiasm inspired us. As a former member of the St. Paul city council and present Ramsey County Commissioner, she could sense what tactics would likely appeal to political newcomers as well as to the more seasoned potential participants. Grassroots campaigning was precisely the technique Hunt employed in all of her successful St. Paul races. She was elated that Minnesota's Groweing would allow women, including herself, to capitalize on their natural networking skills through a political pyramid. (Earlier in the same day, Marie Weiss had decided to drop back a few levels in the pyramid and not to serve on the Committee of 10 — "inclusively" Hunt would be her replacement.)

Of great concern to us all that day was the question of who should comprise the Committee of 100. Mary Vogel-Heffernan talked about the need for "representative constituencies" — women from established networks who could sell the pyramid to their members. We talked about groups we knew — battered women, minorities and, organizations such as Minnesota NOW, Women Against Military Madness (WAMM), the DFL Feminist Caucus, and the American Association of University Women (AAUW). On the one hand, we liked the idea of expanding the pyramid by "planting" a person in each organization who would then work from that group's membership list. Yet the real novelty of our idea, and what we viewed as its simplicity, could be found in the "friend calling 10 friends" process. We finally decided that the Committee of 100 should consist of some leaders from organized groups, but also of women who were good "organizers" in their own right, either in their jobs, their neighborhoods or their churches. We were intent on reaching beyond so-called party "regulars" and in recruiting persons who hitherto may not have been involved in this kind of political process. We wanted women from as many ethnic and racial backgrounds as possible, and we were particularly concerned about including rural women from around the state.

We each described the 10 we had already recruited or planned to recruit. Vogel-Heffernan's and Hunt's lists included women who worked in battered women's shelters, city government, minority aid and rural poverty programs. One of Staples' 10 women was a minister who strongly supported feminism in general and Growe in particular. Barbara Stuhler tapped into her University faculty and staff friends through some of her 10 women. Eight of Linda Holstein's 10 were attorneys. Myrna Marofsky recruited several school teachers and administrators. West said that she would tackle "Greater Minnesota."

Some of our choices had already failed us. When we called women during that first week, we had so little information that we could not give an accurate description of just what Minnesota's Groweing entailed or how much time it would take. The whole concept had been conceived less than a week before, and now we were signing on people for a month and a half commitment. All we could truthfully tell them was how excited we felt and that they would hear the details at a breakfast kickoff on August 9.

Now, we had to hammer out the details. Jean West kept the numbers straight. Was it the Committee of 10,000 who got the shopping bags (we had earlier decided on shopping bags as efficient containers for the kits) or the Committee of 1,000? We spent at least an hour arguing about what should be printed on the signature pages for signing up the voters. Should the volunteers keep one copy and send another to us? We had no office but decided a general post office box was essential. When West recounted her incredible story about ordering buttons and reported that 150,000 were being printed at that very moment, we realized that we had passed the point of no return. Hunt was concerned that the quality of buttons might be inferior, or at least not the vivid green color we had ordered. (West subsequently solved that problem. She recruited one of her Committee of 100 – Alice Keller of Winona – to be an on-site inspector at the printer's to verify the color of the ink. On the following Tuesday, Keller reported that the buttons were "beautiful.") Meanwhile, Stuhler had prepared a draft of the information sheet on Growe and her position on issues. With few changes, it was approved. We had one piece of material ready to go.

On Tuesday morning, July 24, only six days after the first Committee of 10 meeting, some of the 10 met again at Ruby Hunt's over lunch. The big news of the day was a call from LarLu, our button manufacturer. Our hero, Winona Printing, would deliver ahead of schedule, but LarLu needed 50 percent of their $16,000 bill up front with the balance due upon delivery. West called our helpful banker, Gary Woelke, and told him that we needed the money "now . . . please . . . and maybe it should be $25,000 instead of $20,000." A budget had been prepared at the Staples' pool meeting but because we were still uncertain about the quantities and qualities of materials and, because suppliers wanted money upon delivery from a political committee, a little padding beyond our estimated budget seemed advisable. Woelke saw to it that West had all the necessary papers, a fistful of checks, and a note for Stuhler to sign in 15 minutes. The Committee of 10 kept telling Stuhler (who had not volunteered for the honor) how lucky she was to be selected as the member who was allowed to take the risk. There did not seem to be any risk. If only half of the buttons "guaranteed" by the perfect pyramid were paid for, that would be $50,000. Further, we had an extra 50,000 buttons, some of which would certainly be sold by all of those members of the Committee of 10,000 who would get more than their allotted 10 signatures.

It never occurred to the Committee of 10 (soon renamed the "Steering Committee" as the 10s, 100s, 1,000s, 10,000s and 100,000s became more instead of less confusing) that the pyramid would be anything less than near-perfect. We were all getting our 10 and helping our 10 get their 10, and there was very little consideration (at least not verbalized) that this is an imperfect world and all kinds of unexpected contingencies might arise that would result in a substantial shortfall. We gave little thought to the fact that we were in the heighth of the Great Minnesota Vacation Schedule when even the most energetic become slothful. More important, we could not have guessed that when we stated that our $1.00 contribution per button was optional (so as not to prevent any potential Growe supporter from signing up) that so many would indeed pick up that option. So much for the expectation of a $50,000 return to pay our $25,000 note.

Originally, LarLu had promised 112,000 buttons delivered no later than August 7. Remember that we needed 10,000 times 10, 1,000 times 10, and 10 times 100 or 111,000 buttons. But as our organizational details got down on paper, it was very clear that we needed all 150,000 by that date in order to get them into the hands, pockets, and purses of the pyramid participants at the breakfast. Any distribution after the breakfast would be difficult. We had no office, no staff, no telephone—our only lifeline was a P.O.

box number. LarLu was advised that we had underesti-
mated the quantity needed by August 7 and, what was
worse, an August 7 delivery would give us only 36 hours,
working two nights and a day to organize for the breakfast.
LarLu responded without giving us too much hope. If the
weekend was beautiful, there was little chance that a crew
could be enticed to work a weekend shift. If it rained,
LarLu would do its best.

In any event, LarLu would make partial shipments just
as soon as they had buttons ready. On Friday afternoon,
unbelievably, nine days after The First Breakfast and exactly one week after the button copy traveled by bus to Winona, we were advised that the first shipment of buttons
was ready. But they did not know if they could catch the air
express driver who made daily runs to the Minneapolis-St.
Paul airport. They could not locate him.

As West remembers it:

*"Knowing there were buttons finished, I had to have
them. I couldn't stand the suspense of waiting until a
Monday evening delivery. There had to be a way to get
those buttons. If I got in my car and raced to Winona,
there would be no one to open the shipping department for me. I asked if they could be put on a bus. No,
the last bus that day was leaving in 15 minutes. Could
they call the bus depot and hold the bus? For political
buttons and for some nutty, persistent woman who
kept calling every 10 minutes trying to figure out a
way? I knew there was a way. I just didn't know what
it was. The buttons were there. They were boxed to
go. But no one was there to sign the shipping papers.
And the boxes did not have wings. It was hot and getting late and I was dejected and frustrated and ready
for a large, cool drink. And then LarLu called. One of
their employees lived in Minneapolis and would pack
as many boxes in his small car as he could and would
call me from a hotel on the freeway outside of town as*

*soon as he arrived. I went home and had the drink.
Smiling, I waited for the call."*

At 7:30 P.M. box after box came out of that helpful employee's small car and was transferred to West's station wagon. The first shipment of buttons had arrived! Seventeen cartons each containing four plastic bags of 500 buttons each were carried into the Stuhler/West front hall. They were beautiful — the printing and fabrication excellent. The numbers printed on the buttons were sequential in each bag — sequential in lots of 500. West pulled out a bag. The numbers were 132,501 to 133,000. The numbers on the buttons were special . . . our distinguishing feature. But if we put just any 10 buttons in a kit, we would lose the effectiveness of the gimmick of having them numbered. There was a place on the signature sheet for the button number opposite the name of the voter who got the button. If the buttons were sequential in each kit, it would add importance to filling out the sheet properly and appear that each voter would be recorded somewhere. We would be able to count the exact number from the careful tabulation of button numbers. Yes. There was no question. Each 10 buttons in each kit had to be in sequence in order to make it appear that each of the 150,000 buttons were going to be accounted for. Somebody was keeping track! Never mind that we weren't. That was it then. The bags of 500 buttons would have to be opened and sorted, one by one.

West opened a bag, had another drink and with some enthusiasm put 500 buttons in numerical sequence on the floor. By the time she had assembled the second bag, she had determined that it would take anywhere from one hour (barely possible) to two hours per bag of 500, depending on the sorter's agility and dedication, to sort by number and package each 10 buttons in a little Baggie and repack each 500 sack with 50 little Baggies preparatory to stuffing the 11,110 kits. It was summer. There had to be SOME kids left in town willing to earn one cent per button — $2.50 an hour up to a questionable $5.00 an hour for the highly motivated — but who might they be? West went to the store the next day for more Baggies and continued to assemble buttons throughout the weekend.

The next meeting of the Steering Committee was the following Monday night, and most of the members went home with more than one box of 2,000 buttons to assemble. But the word of the potential for income for skis, bikes, and stereo equipment travelled fastest to the Vogel-Heffernan household where three teen-age boys spent the better part of many days and nights sorting and bagging buttons. Three hundred bags of buttons would mean 450 or more hours of labor and an additional budget item of $1,500 — less the few bags that Committee members had time to do themselves. An expensive time-consuming gimmick indeed.

At the same time the button adventure was underway, other materials had to be developed. A memorandum of instructions along with a checklist of things to do and a calendar were sent to the Committee of 100 on July 25. That was the group that had to be up and running and in the process of recruiting the next layer of the pyramid. After that, the kit of materials for the Committee of 10,000 and a master kit for the Committee of 1,000 had to be prepared. We had finally determined that the kit for the 10,000 with instructions printed on the manila envelope should include 10 or more copies of the information sheet on Growe, not one but two signature sheets, and 10 buttons (although the 10,000 were supposed to sign up 10, we hoped the additional materials would encourage them to do more — and, in fact, many did). The kit for the 1,000 included all of the above as well as a memorandum of instructions and a timetable. Most of these materials were created by West who could keep the complications straight and by Stuhler who tried to put them in the simplist possible terms. (See the Appendices for copies.) Thanks to Jerry McCarthy, the printer, the hundreds of boxes of these materials were delivered to an empty room in West's office building on July 31 — we had eight days to put them all together in shopping bags (with an appropriate green stripe down the sides) which had been acquired by Ruby Hunt. Thanks to West's landlord, Jim Gardner, owner of the Finch Building in Lowertown, St. Paul, we were able to have space, light, and enjoy air conditioning, even on nights and weekends at only a nominal charge.

From Tuesday, July 31 through August 8 members of the Steering Committee, friends, and relatives worked to assemble the materials. We had to pick up the forms and one Baggie of buttons and stuff them into the manila envelope. There were to be 11 kits in each shopping bag—one for the member of the Committee of 1,000 and one for each of the 10 in her pyramid—the Committee of 10,000. There would be kits also for the Committee of 100 and the Steering Committee. There would be 11,110 kits in all. We worked night and day and all weekend. It was not exactly "blood, sweat, and tears," but it was close. Whenever our spirits sagged, West would break into song. "Are you havin' any fun? What y' gettin' out of' living? What good is what you've got—if you're not—havin' any fun?"[3] Despite the theme song she provided for Minnesota's Groweing, it was still not anyone's favorite activity, but we kept going with the aid of soft drinks, chips, a few witticisms and, most of all, by the consuming idea that had brought us together in the first place—to put Joan Growe into the U.S. Senate. Incredibly, we got the job done (with a few clean-up chores still uncompleted) in time for the breakfast that was to launch the Minnesota's Groweing campaign. From Saturday, July 14 to Wednesday, August 9—or in less than four weeks—we had put together a full-fledged campaign organization complete with mission and materials.

The morning of August 9, 1984 started for all of us at 5:30 A.M. at the Prom Center. After much discussion, we had hired two large semi-trailers to haul the shopping bags filled with kits from the Finch building to the Prom Center, a distance of approximately four miles. We earlier rejected the possibility of transferring the bags ourselves when we saw how much floor space they occupied. It would have taken us an enormous amount of total driving time that we could ill-afford. Mary Vogel-Heffernan's three sons and other younger workers had painstakingly put all the buttons in order and packed them in plastic bags. Their final task was to load the trucks the afternoon before the breakfast and help unload them in the faint light of dawn on the morning of August 9.

Each of the 10 members of the Steering Committee, in addition to helping the boys unload the trucks at the Prom Center, had specific tasks for the breakfast. Ruby Hunt, who was the efficiency expert in the assembling process and who had spent almost 30 hours stuffing bags at the Finch Building, also managed to find a printer at the last minute to make a big Minnesota's Groweing banner. Myrna Marofsky, the treasurer of Minnesota's Groweing, took charge of registering every woman who attended—and made sure they each paid $5.00. Kathleen Scott, who was in charge of arrangements, interrupted her vacation to attend the event.

Martie Norton volunteered for what she foresaw as a relatively simple, enjoyable task: filling 200 balloons with helium and affixing them to 72 tables. The night before the breakfast, Norton picked up a large helium tank and the requisite number of balloons. She arrived at the Prom Center shortly before 6:00 A.M., which gave her more than an hour to pop the tank, blow up and distribute the balloons. Unfortunately, she had forgotten a tool with which to dislodge the cap on the tank. Panic struck. How could we pretend to have a political event without balloons? After a fruitless trip by Norton to the near-by Vogel-Heffernan household in search of an appropriate gadget, the semi-truck driver found some tool resembling a wrench from his cab and uncorked the helium tank. We had gas. As hundreds of women started to coverge on the registration table, Norton hurridly filled the balloons, and we rushed them into the dining room, letting some — in our exuberance — fly to the ceiling. Norton relaxed.

While that tense operation was going on, West tested the microphone. It was not your ordinary "one, two three, testing." Instead it was our theme song. Staples and Greenman rushed to join her, and we were treated to a spirited rendition of "Are You Havin' Any Fun?"

When the 100, 1,000 and even some 10,000 committee members began to arrive on that lovely August morning, we realized people did not know where they were supposed to sit. We had organized tables in rows, according to the 10 members of the Steering Committee. For example, each woman from Virginia Greenman's Committee of 100 had a table, at which were seated 10 more women they had invited. These latter women were members of the Committee of 1,000. Individual Steering Committee members had no idea who their 10 had recruited for their 10. There hadn't been time to obtain that information, much less "chart" it for the breakfast. Another problem surfaced — for some inscrutable reason, the Prom Center waitresses refused to serve coffee "until everyone was seated." Kathleen Scott, in charge of the arrangements, was dumbfounded.

Emily Staples had been assigned the job of convincing the press that our breakfast was a newsworthy event. A news release had been issued, and we benefited from a *Minneapolis Tribune* article by reporter Lori Sturdevant on August 8. It detailed our reasons for starting the pyramid and what we expected to accomplish on the kickoff the next day. The story made us legitimate. On the morning Sturdevant's article appeared, the Steering Committee met for breakfast at the Normandy Hotel in Minneapolis. Between reading parts of the story aloud to each other, we joked about various lines we might use at the kickoff. Stuhler said she had recently heard a pithy analysis of why women generally make better workers than men — her remark, "the rooster crows but the hens deliver" became the punchline of Holstein's speech to the gathering the next day. It caught the attention of Bill Salisbury from the *St. Paul Pioneer Press* and of both WCCO-TV and KSTP-TV. More importantly, the line appealed to all the women who came to breakfast not only out of loyalty to the person who had recruited them but because they believed that a solidified female vote could stop Mattson cold. Staples got the press there, and they went away impressed with the breadth of support for Growe's candidacy.

Joan Growe was not the first speaker at the breakfast. It fell to Jean West to explain the pyramid and all of its attendant processes in less than 10 minutes. Sounding more reasonable than she did with her Steering Committee colleagues who failed to master all the intricacies of the organization, West implored the group to read the directions and, if there were any questions, their recruiter or contact person should be able to answer them (or so we devoutly hoped).

At approximately 8:15 A.M., Barbara Stuhler introduced several women elected officials among those present and then turned to the introduction of Joan Growe. As she finished, Virginia Greenman said that she could feel the room levitate, and Growe was given a standing ovation as she walked to the platform. That kind of enthusiastic response continued throughout Growe's speech. She was visibly affected by the crowd's affirmation, probably because although she knew of our existence and our intentions, she really had no intimate knowledge of what we were all about, a condition dictated more by law than by her own inclination.

Following Growe's well-received speech, Holstein who was presiding over the event pinned button Number 1 on her. In turn, Growe handed her $1.00 (slipped to her in advance by Vogel-Heffernan). Although that symbolic exchange was meant to illustrate that the buttons were not to be given away, the message was not strong enough. Because we had decided to suggest — but not require — a contribution of $1.00 for each button, language to that effect was printed on our literature. That fundamental error continued to haunt us.

We had arranged for a photographer to take pictures of Joan Growe with out-state members of the pyramid after the breakfast. She graciously posed for several photographs and thanked us again for our efforts. By 9:15 A.M., the room was empty, both of people and of the 1,000 shopping bags. (Later we would learn that one of Marofsky's "10," on an errand for her church after the breakfast, went to a jail to pick up a bag lady and take her to a shelter. After delivering her passenger, the woman drove home and then discovered that her bag lady had acquired another possession — a Minnesota's Groweing bag.) The Steering Committee sat down to count our breakfast money and hand-endorse each $5.00 check. At 10:00 A.M., we all left for our respective jobs or other responsibilities. It had been an incredible week. It had already been an incredible day.

When 500 women walked into the Prom Center that morning, they saw a room filled with 72 tables, a large Minnesota's Groweing banner, and balloons, balloons, balloons. Miraculously, the sound system worked perfectly, the bags left the room, and the nucleus of the pyramid organization had been imbued, if not with total clarity, with more than ample enthusiasm. We were elated. We had had barely four weeks to plan the entire event but we seemed to have pulled it off quite smoothly. We had captured, at least for one day in August, the well-documented but short-lived mood among voters that this was the year of the woman in American politics. The selection of Geraldine Ferraro as Mondale's running mate in mid-July, the announcement at Minnesota's State Capitol, and the enthusiastic reception of Ferraro at the Democratic National Convention, left supporters of Joan Growe with a renewed sense of hope and excitement. And now the pyramid was ready to "growe."

While the Steering Committee members took a brief respite from the mobilization of Minnesota's Groweing, the pyramid began to take shape. Although many of the Committee of 100 had already recruited their 10 (the Committee of 1,000) and some of those their 10 (the Committee of 10,000), their efforts now began in earnest. And so did the task of the 10,000 to sign up their 10 — the 100,000 who would vote for Growe in the primary. After a week or so, the returns began to come in. Each day, West stopped at P.O. Box 75700 in the St. Paul Post Office and collected the mail. Each night Stuhler worked with West, counting the signatures and the money, endorsing checks (by this time we had a stamp for deposit), and making out deposit slips. The mail was substantial but it never reached the proportions we had envisioned. We had dreamed of a P.O. Box overflowing but it never did. As time went on, we began to realize that our emphasis on signatures over money was not producing the income we anticipated. There were cheers when unexpected big checks came in, but they were never numerous enough to offset the returns that contained no money at all. Many, of course, were right on with 10 names and 10 dollars. We enjoyed the occasional notes:

> *From Carol Flavin* — "*I did it! Got my 10. I'm glad I did this — thanks for the opportunity.*"
> *From Nancy Goseholt* — "*Thanks for the great idea and organization.*"
> *From Shirley Holm* — "*Thank you very much for getting this effort off the ground — onward to success in September — and November.*"
> *From Ellen Johnson* — "*Hope all is going strong.*"

On August 22, 13 days after the kickoff breakfast, the Steering Committee was back at work. That noon, Holstein, Staples, Stuhler and West met at the Minneapolis Athletic Club with Growe's campaign manager, Steve Novak, and Floyd F. Fithian, finance chair of the Democratic Senatorial Campaign Committee. The purpose of the meeting — at least it was Novak's purpose — was to inform Fithian of all the dimensions of the Growe campaign. Even in its early stages, Minnesota's Groweing, although a separate organization, was important to that campaign and to the prospects for a generous contribution from the well-endowed group represented by Fithian, but Fithian seemed more interested in describing the Democratic Senatorial Campaign Committee's processes and providing anecdotal political information than in hearing about the role of Minnesota's Groweing.[4]

That same evening, the Steering Committee met at the home shared by West and Stuhler at 130 Prospect Boulevard in St. Paul. This had become the customary meeting place. Of all the decisions we had to make, this was not one of them as gathering at "130" became an accepted habit. That night — even before the primary election — we struggled with our after-the-primary future. We finally agreed that we should meet with the Committee of 100 in order to broaden the base of participation and get some new ideas. The meeting would be in the Campus Club at the University of Minnesota from 4:30 to 6:00 P.M. on Tuesday, September 4, the day after Labor Day. We sent out double postcards announcing the event and providing a return card for reservations.

We also discussed attending special activities where a ready-made crowd would be present. Ruby Hunt, an experienced hand at working crowds, was the enthusiast for this approach — others of the Committee were more hesitant. On September 1, a rainy Saturday morning, Hunt, Stuhler and West showed up at St. Paul's famous outdoor Farmers Market with bags of buttons, materials and homemade Minnesota's Groweing signs. Hunt was the star stopper and recruiter — many left not only with buttons but with signature sheets as well. Stuhler left after a bit for another appointment but Hunt and West continued peddling Minnesota's Groweing until well beyond the noon hour. That, however, was pretty much the extent of our bravado in public gatherings.

The meeting at the Campus Club on Tuesday, September

4 was attended by over 30 women of the committee of 100, a good turnout for the day after the summer's last long weekend. There were mixed messages except for one. Everyone agreed that Minnesota's Groweing should keep going after the primary. But the direction was never clearly set — or at least there was no consensus on how best to proceed. The Steering Committee gathered afterwards at Grandma's, a dining and drinking establishment on the West Bank of the University's campus. We still could not agree on a course of action. But if the future of Minnesota's Groweing was unknown, the present was very clear. We were confident that Joan Growe would win the Primary election and that we had contributed in a significant way to that happy prospect.

5 | The Outcome

"GROWE THRASHES MATTSON."[1] That one headline said it all! By God we had done it! All those hours of meetings, all those dreary and crazy days, all those weeks of determination had paid off. We had helped Joan Growe win a smashing victory over Bob Mattson in the primary election.

There were significant elements in Growe's success. She had out-organized, out-spent, and out-hustled Mattson. She had campaigned throughout the state for many months. She had spent over half a million dollars. During the week before the primary, 750,000 pieces of Growe literature were distributed, and 9,000 lawn signs were implanted. She had also benefited from the largest-ever DFL voter identification effort and get-out-the-vote drive.[2] The revelations by the *Minneapolis Star and Tribune* a week before the primary of Mattson's financial dealings in Florida with their attendant debts and bankruptcies certainly did not help his cause.[3] Mattson, who had hoped to carry his native Eighth Congressional District, had campaigned on old issues — the Boundary Waters Canoe Area and gun control. But there were new issues and new concerns. The famous Mesabi Range which had produced iron ore for the steel mills of the nation was severely depressed as the demand for domestic steel was down and, consequently, unemployment in the region was rampant. The Executive Director of the local United Steel Workers Union said, "We're down so bad now we can't worry about the BWCA or gun control. Up here people are worried about where they are going to work. The issue is jobs."[4] Growe was in tune with that mood. "I can't believe that the people of northern Minnesota who care so much about jobs and employment are going to vote for someone who was elected to public office and didn't bother to show up for work," she said, referring to Mattson's prolonged stay in Florida early in his term.[5] Growe carried all 87 Minnesota counties and all but one precinct in winning over Mattson by a margin of 76 to 20 percent (the vote was 238,190 for Growe, 61,489 for Mattson, and 14,251 for seven other candidates).[6]

And what part did Minnesota's Groweing play in the outcome of the primary? It is difficult to say with any precision. We do know, however, that pyramid representatives could be found in 283 communities outside the metropolitan area (see Appendix B for location of the communities and Appendix C for the list). We covered the state from Ada to Zumbrota, from Grand Portage to Caledonia, from Afton to Morris, and from East Grand Forks to Pipestone. Minnesota's Groweing was there!

Some notes that came in with the signature sheets to P.O. Box 75700 in St. Paul tell the story:

> *From Helen Rudie in Moorhead: "If responses of people I contacted were typical, the campaign really did increase the number of persons who voted last Tuesday."*
> *From Heather Ferguson of St. Olaf Democrats: "Here are the lists and donations from St. Olaf College. We turned out 60 votes for Joan Growe after having been on campus just one week. Keep up the good work."*
> *From Shellie Kromminga in Glencoe: "I attended the kickoff breakfast for the project although I did not have a contact at the time. I took [away] with me a*

shopping bag (I guess I'm one of the Committee of 1,000) and have recruited 10 volunteers who each received their kit. Please assign a pyramid contact to me, if possible. Thanks."
From Betty Lavicky in Spring Valley: *not a note but a sticker with a very happy tortoise on skates and "way to go" on his shell.*

A few days before the primary, Lori Sturdevant, writing in the *Minneapolis Star and Tribune*, noted that the Growe-Mattson contest had not turned out to be much of a barn-burner. Growe was favored to win because she had her party's endorsement, a $600,000 campaign fund, TV advertising, and help from an independent get-out-the-vote telephone pyramid. That "telephone pyramid," of course, was Minnesota's Groweing.[7] Our instruction sheets asked everyone in the pyramid orgaization to call their 10 just before primary day, reminding everyone to go to the polls.

We are confident that Minnesota's Groweing did help swell the Growe vote on September 11, 1984. Even more important, however, it was the impetus for the first–time involvement of many women — and probably some men — in the political process. This was the kind of door-opening that women candidates like Growe inspired even if those candidates ultimately lost. Minnesota's Groweing provided women and men who care about good politics with a tangible opportunity to express their enthusiasm for a woman candidate above and beyond their votes at the polls.

As usual, the press had its say. An editorial in the *St. Paul Dispatch* commented that "Her margin was space-age, but in truth there is uncertainty whether the voters were expressing their confidence in Mrs. Growe as much as their lack of confidence in Mr. Mattson. Probably some of both." The editorial continued:

"She battled tenaciously and effectively to win her party's endorsement at a divided state convention in June. Equally as important, she has been impressive in

*her chipping away at doubts about her ability to deal
with national and international issues; she earned the
chance to test her views and her appeal to the voters
against Mr. Boschwitz."*[8]

But the *Minneapolis Star and Tribune* across the river did
not entirely share that assessment. It began on a similar
note but with a different conclusion:

*"Joan Growe is the bright star of Tuesday's primary
election. . . . With a dozen years in public office,
with one and a half years already spent campaigning
and with support from the Democratic Senatorial
Campaign Committee, her latest victory is just one
more asset in an array so impressive that only a spoilsport would point to the liabilities. Call us a
spoilsport."*

After pointing to the awesome Boschwitz campaign chest
and Growe's tendency "to turn tough issues into jelly," the
editorial warned:

*"Growe has persevered in a long campaign. She has
shown great empathy for Minnesotans and their problems. She has identified important issues on which she
and Boschwitz differ. We look forward to hearing her
clarify her views. If she does not, the bright star will
fade."*[9]

In the aftermath of Joan Growe's victory, the Steering
Committee of Minnesota's Groweing savored its success.
We met again the evening of September 12 and contemplated next steps. The group was ambivalent. Our reason
for being was to put Joan Growe into the United States Senate, yes, but our energies had all been targeted on the primary election. The Mattson challenge had been the chief
cause of our organization. We never had time to think
about the general election except in a peripheral way—we

had not plotted any long-range strategy. We were so preoccupied with things of the moment that there would have been no time — however much we might have wanted it — to have a game plan in hand.

There were some things we knew. Incumbent Rudy Boschwitz in the general election was going to be a far more formidable opponent than Bob Mattson in the primary election. In the years prior to his going to the U.S. Senate, Boschwitz had made his company, Plywood Minnesota, a household name. Like Lee Iaccoca of Chrysler, he had made his presence known to Minnesotans by advertising on television. Unlike Iaccoca whose presence is clearly corporate, Boschwitz was customarily clad in an open-necked plaid shirt. His manner was gentle and folksy. Though he had been active in politics, serving as Republican National Committeeman from 1971 to 1978, Boschwitz had never held public office until his successful bid for the Senate in 1978. He won over incumbent Senator Wendell R. Anderson whose incumbency — or the manner by which he achieved it — turned out to be the decisive issue of that campaign.

Ironically, Boschwitz's election to the Senate was facilitated by the election of Walter F. Mondale to the vice presidency of the United States in 1976. Mondale was the second Minnesotan, after his friend and mentor, Hubert H. Humphrey, to occupy the nation's second highest position. On December 29 of that year, Wendell Anderson resigned as Governor midway in his second term. The next day — on December 30 — Lieutenant Governor Rudy Perpich succeeded to the governorship; Mondale, preparing to asume office as Vice President, resigned his Senate seat, and Perpich appointed Anderson to succeed him.[10] Although Anderson had been a popular, attractive, and effective governor, this power-play (or so it was perceived) was not kindly received by Minnesota voters who rejected his bid for election in favor of Boschwitz on November 7, 1978. There were seven contenders for the open Senate seat in that election; Boschwitz received 56.6 percent of the vote and Anderson 40.4 percent.[11]

The new Minnesota Senator caused something of a stir on the Washington scene. His informal dress (although he did wear a tie in the Senate) and relaxed manner were anomalies among his more traditionally clad and intense colleagues. Some observers believe that Boschwitz was an indifferent Senator in the early years of his incumbency, and it was only in the year prior to the 1984 election that he began to make much of a mark and tend to his fences back home.[12]

Rudy Boschwitz had several credits in his political ledger. He was a Republican incumbent in what turned out to be a very good year for Republicans and especially for incumbents. He was an effective campaigner and generally regarded as a "nice guy." He was a Jew, and the Jewish community could count on his representing Israel's interests in senatorial debates. Some Jewish women, however, parted company with him because of his opposition to the pro-choice position.[13] There were many who otherwise might have been expected to be in the Growe camp but they were not — the issue of Israel was simply too compelling. He was, important to Minnesota, a member of the Senate Agricultural Committee. He was generally supportive of the Reagan administration's foreign policy although he was beginning to differ in some respects on Central American issues. It was important to some communities — including the Jewish community — that he opposed the President's advocacy of prayer in the schools.

On the other side of the coin, his votes for nerve gas and the MX missile evoked criticism from women and from those associated with the nuclear freeze movement. His record on social security, his opposition to the Equal Rights Amendment and other issues dear to the hearts of feminists, and his votes on environmental legislation were legitimate issues for contention. None of them, however, proved decisive. In the end, the main message of Growe's campaign against Boschwitz — or the public memory that will linger on — was more negative than positive. While Growe easily found areas of disagreement with her opponent on a wide range of substantive issues, none of them took off or, as one reporter put it, was "a real grabber."[14] Growe's persistent insistence that Boschwitz make public his income tax returns and his refusal to do so did not generate the expected sense of public outrage. His support of a controversial products liability bill that could possibly profit his own business also failed to produce a ground swell of protest.[15] Even his refusal to take a no-cut pledge on social security could not sway the voters. Mostly, the image of "nice guy" Rudy overcame any of Growe's efforts to demonstrate their differences and why the voters should choose her over him. Finally, it must be said that the phenomenon that affected the nation was also present in Minnesota. Never mind the candidates' positions — what mattered in the polling place was the people's perception that the nation was on the right course. It was, despite serious differences with the Soviet Union and intractable conflicts in Central America and the Middle East, at peace. It was, despite a devastating federal deficit — and persistent poverty for some — experiencing economic recovery.

But we are getting ahead of our story. If we knew Boschwitz was going to be a formidable opponent, we were also apprehensive because the Mondale campaign had not achieved any real momentum. The excitement of the Democratic Convention in San Francisco had paled in the weeks since mid-July. Mondale seemed to be on a plateau. Ferraro's problems with family business finances had seemingly been resolved with her impressive two-and-a-half hour news conference on Tuesday, August 21. But questions remained.

The Steering Committe had believed that Growe would benefit with a fellow-Minnesotan heading the ticket. We were not the only ones with that opinion. When Mondale was the vice presidential nominee in 1976, the number of Minnesota voters increased by 200,000. Mary Monohan, state DFL chair, estimated that there would be an additional 300,000 to 400,000 voters who would help elect Joan Growe and other DFL candidates.[16] Or, as Ellen Goodman wrote in the late stages of the campaign, "The gender gap is probably less important than the funding gap or, for that matter, the national ticket gap. Joan Growe's chance to close in, to become 'the woman' in the fading 'year of the woman' may finally depend on how well Mondale does in his home state."[17]

But then there was Geraldine Ferraro. A headline at the time of the announcement of Mondale's choice of his running mate said it all, "Ferraro adds fire to Fritz."[18] Even with the difficulties surrounding her husband's business affairs, Ferraro was clearly the most exciting and visible figure on the Democratic ticket. Her appearances drew enthusiastic crowds (and pro-life hecklers as well). To the Steering Committee, the vice presidential nominee seemed the best ace up our collective sleeve. A Ferraro-Growe rally could reinvigorate the campaign. We were confident it would energize women of Minncsota for the remaining weeks of our efforts to elect Growe to the Senate.

The thought was not a new one. We had talked about it before the primary but now it took on a certain urgency. Members of the Committee kept pressing the matter with staff at Growe headquarters who, needless to say, were enthusiastic, and with the national campaign office as well where scheduling priorities were being worked out. Suddenly, the hoped-for Ferraro appearance was promised, and Minnesota's Groweing learned a lot about how fast a rally and a fund-raiser can be pasted together. Lieutenant Governor Marlene Johnson and Nancy Farnham organized what turned out to be a historic fund-raising event. They had recruited a group of about 125 women who would ask others to pay either $1000 or $100 to the Democratic Victory Fund which was the vehicle for the national registration drive. Those paying $1,000 would have a chance to meet Ferraro and have their picture taken with her. Those paying $100 would also have a chance to hear her. It was a kind of friendly "upstairs-downstairs" happening at the St. Paul Athletic Club following the late afternoon rally.

Meanwhile, Minnesota's Groweing had been selected as the contact for the rally scheduled for Wednesday, September 19.[19] In the wee small hours on Saturday morning, September 15, Lynn Christianson, a Ferraro advance worker from St. Charles, Illinois arrived in St. Paul. (Little did she know when she arrived wearing a souvenir of a previous political forray — a "Big Red" sweatshirt from the University of Nebraska — that this was the weekend of the Minnesota-Nebraska football game until a fellow-traveler pointed out the error of her ways.) Later that morning, Barbara Stuhler and Jean West picked up her at the Hotel St. Paul to tour prospective rally sites in Minneapolis. After weighing the pros and cons of three viable possibilities and a call to campaign headquarters in Washington D.C., Christianson made the decision to hold the event in a park-like setting on the north side of the Hennepin Government Center (if it rained, we could move inside).

On Sunday, West again drove Christianson who had been joined by two other recently arrived Mondale-Ferraro workers to review the site and then they parted company. The nitty-gritty responsibilities of making the rally go would rest with the Christianson advance team. Minnesota's Groweing would activate the pyramid to inform those who had "signed up for Growe" that anyone wearing a Groweing button would be able to get into the special section cordoned off for various and sundry V.I.P.s.

The day of the rally was beautiful. Linda Holstein and Jean West from the Steering Committee were on the platform. John Derus, the Hennepin County Commissioner who had been one of Growe's contenders for the endorsement, introduced the dignitaries. DFL politicians were all there: the Congressional delegation, the mayors of Minneapolis and St, Paul, legislators, and other party leaders. Holstein and West were introduced, and Holstein spoke for Minnesota's Groweing, "Thank you to all who are wearing a green and white button. Joan won with 76 percent in the primary. We did it then and we are going for it again on November 6."

Finally, Ferraro, who was running about an hour behind time, arrived to a delirium of cheers and waving banners. Reports estimated a crowd of 7,000.[20] Growe introduced Ferraro and pinned our button on her saying, "We have a little bit of magic here called "Minnesota's Groweing" and noted that it represented one of the largest, most effective volunteer campaign efforts in the country. Those wearing their buttons visibly swelled with pride and a sense of accomplishment. (Holstein had been anxious during the wait, repeatedly asking West, "Are you sure Joan's got the button, are you sure?" West had entrusted the button to Growe's son, David, and although Holstein continued to worry that the button would be lost in transition, it was not.) Ferraro gave a short but captivating talk and then plunged into the crowd to shake hands with some of those standing nearby.

Then she was off to the St. Paul Athletic Club and the fund-raising events. The pro-life partisans were out in force, and people had to thread their way through a police line to get into the building. (Fortunately, except for a minor skirmish between one pro-lifer and a network cameraman, nothing untoward occured. Later, on the plane, Ferraro greeted him as "my hero" and supplied him with an ice pack.)[21] Ferraro spoke first to the $1,000 contributors and then had to speak in two different rooms to accommodate the hundreds of $100 contributors. More than a quarter of a million dollars was raised, the largest single money event in DFL history. This was still another encouraging sign that women were becoming increasingly adept at the money side of politics. Lieutenant Governor Marlene Johnson, one of the event's organizers, was quoted as saying, "Geraldine Ferraro's candidacy is a message that this country is ready for shared leadership and shared responsibility in public-policy making. Now those of us in local leadership have an opportunity to put our money where our mouths are and show that we know she makes a difference to what women believe they can really do."[22]

Despite the crowded elevators and clogged stairways that would have strained almost anyone's good humor, there was euphoria in the air. Minnesota's Groweing buttons were everywhere to be seen and so, too, were some notable Republican women. Ferraro meant something to these Minnesota women and the daughters they brought with them — another milestone on the path to equality. The fact that there were too many people in too small a place simply could not diminsh that feeling of well-being and happiness. "Gerry, Gerry, Gerry" — she had them with her every step of the way and then, for Geraldine Ferraro, it was another plane ride and another rally.

As Ferraro was leaving the Athletic Club, Jean West saw one of the advance men working with Lynn Christianson and said, "Bill, I'd really like to meet *her*." Bill said "sure" and positioned her on Ferraro's exit route down some back stairs. When Christianson, who was with the candidate, saw West, she said to Ferraro, "There's one more person I'd like you to meet" and introduced them. West, whose hair — though gray — is not unlike Ferraro's, said she was working on a Ferraro cut. Whereupon the candidate reported that the last time she had her hair done, her hairdresser finished with a flourish and observed, "There — you look just like Geraldine Ferraro." And then she was gone, leaving behind an absolutely charmed Steering Committee member.

The Ferraro rally was now history and, once again the Steering Committee convened at the West-Stuhler residence in St. Paul. We drew from the ranks of the Committee of 100 Joan Campbell, an administrator at the University of Minnesota hospitals, Ellen Hartnett, a social worker, Debra Page, a Minneapolis lawyer, and Martha Platt, a community activist. Each of them had been effective recruiters and organizers and were identified as good prospects for an infusion of ideas and energy. Both Hartnett and Platt were present for the meeting on Tuesday, September 25.

Many of us had been asked, "What should we do now?" "Where do we go from here?" "What are your plans?" Expanding the pyramid from 100,000 to 1,000,000 was one. But such an expansion, given what we already knew about the weak links in the chain of communication and performance, seemed an unreasonable and unworkable activity. We were also facing the prospects of a debt. Because money was still coming in, we were unsure of its final dimensions. We had excess buttons as pyramiders were beginning to return unused materials but there seemed no viable way to use them except as those in the pyramid continued to sign up voters for Growe which some did indeed do. Finally, after exploring these and other options, we agreed to spend money in order to communicate with other potential voters and to generate additional income. In part because the Growe campaign was not using them, we decided to have postcards printed and include samples in a letter to the Committees of 100 and 1,000 asking them to do four things: 1) to continue selling the buttons; 2) to purchase and send out the new postcards; 3) speak up for Growe and her positions, and 4) to send in money already contributed and to make new individual contributions.

We did succeed in getting some of that money that we knew was lying around in purses and desk drawers. Some individuals did send us contributions, and those were often generous contributions. The postcards were a flop! Actually, they were probably the most attractive piece of material we produced in the campaign. Linda Wood, a graphic designer, volunteered her services and gave us a Minnesota's Groweing button with the number 1,000,000 on the front side. Wood also rescued the button from confusion by doing it this way—MINNESOTA'S GROWEing so the Growe stood out and the message became more clear. On the back, we printed "Remember to vote for Joan Growe on November 6. Your vote *will* make a difference." Although postcards have been a common device in political campaigns, they were — we later realized — redundant in the context of a pyramid organization where so many women and men had already communicated with the voters they knew and some they may not have known. To be sure, there were some purchases but we gave hundreds of cards away, preferring to have them out there rather than sitting on a shelf unused. That mailing together with the cost of the postcards and letter and other minor post-primary expenses added nearly $1,900 to our debt.

Members of the Steering Committee met on Sunday and Monday, October 21 and 22 to address the envelopes and get out the mailing. The dining room at 130 Prospect Blvd. was turned into an addressing and assembling operation. We were later than planned with the distribution because the postcard took longer to prepare and print than we had anticipated. By the time the Committees had received them, the election was only two weeks away.

There were other last minute efforts. Minnesota's Groweing booked a booth at the convention of the Minnesota Education Association in the Minneapolis Auditorium. Steering Committee members Greenman, Holstein, Hunt, Marofsky, Norton, Staples and West were joined by Ellen Hartnett and Sue Mavorec to distribute buttons and postcards to interested teachers. They were somewhat surprised to find — given the endorsement of the national Democratic ticket by the National Education Association, the endorsement of Growe by the MEA, and the fact that Growe herself was a former teacher — that not all MEA members were Growe enthusiasts. Incidentally, Growe won the MEA endorsement from Boschwitz even though in 1978, the MEA had chosen Boschwitz over Anderson.[23]

On Monday, October 29, a phone bank was organized. Myrna Marofsky recruited some callers, and four other members of the Steering Committee came to West's office to

use the phones there. Their message was a simple one —
vote, call your 10, have them call their 10, send in button
money, send in money, vote for Joan Growe.

On Tuesday, October 30, Committee members Holstein,
Stuhler and West were interviewed by National Public Radio. Most of the discussion addressed Growe's chances of
winning and the extent to which the "women's vote" would
be a strategic factor in determining the outcome of the
Mondale-Ferraro and Growe-Boschwitz races. Holstein and
Stuhler voiced their concerns that younger women, especially professional and business women in their twenties
and thirties, apparently did not identify with Growe's personal and professional struggles. To West, it seemed that
Growe had overcome tremendous odds to achieve success
and recognition as a viable political candidate. While all
three agreed that Minnesota's Groweing was ample evi-
dence of women's support, we could not predict with any
certainty how women might vote in this election. There was
too little attention to women's issues as such and too many
other factors that would determine the final outcome. The
interview, however, was still another indication that Minnesota's Groweing was making its mark as an effective separate
campaign instrument beyond the boundaries of the state.

And then there was the news conference when nobody
came. The announcement went out: "Minnesota's Groweing, the independent, volunteer committee organized
primarily to insure a significant women's vote for Joan
Growe will hold a press conference tomorrow (Thursday,
November 1) at the Minneapolis Club." The place was
selected because that had been the official origination site of
Minnesota's Groweing two-and-a-half months before. The
purpose was to report on our post-primary activities, to say
something about the national response to the pyramid idea,
and to address the charge that Growe had been "too tough"
in her campaign against Rudy Boschwitz. In a recent full-
page ad, Senator David Durenberger had charged, "Mrs.

Growe, you've gone too far" and then went on to castigate her for not campaigning in the Minnesota tradition. Never mind that campaigns in Minnesota have sometimes failed to illuminate the issues and have been the occasion for charges and allegations sometimes unsubstantiated. It is true that we take pride in the Minnesota political tradition, but that tradition is distinguished by the strength of the two major parties, by the calibre of many of those elected to public office, and by high voter turnout. It is worth speculating whether or not such a condescending and patronizing political ad would have been directed towards a male candidate.

In any event, Steering Committee members gathered a bit before 1:00 P.M., hung the banner with the replication of the green and white Minnesota's Groweing button numbered 100,000, and waited for representatives of the news organizations to arrive. B. J. Mahling came from Growe headquarters with a tape recorder but nobody else did. Steering Committee members, good-humored even in adversity, persuaded Linda Holstein to make her presentation. The content of Holstein's statement was upbeat:

> *"At the time we formed Minnesota's Groweing, Joan Growe was 22 points behind Rudy Boschwitz. . . . The latest poll says she's behind by seven points among those most likely to vote. We think women are particularly likely to vote in this election, especially in Minnesota. . . . Our pyramid has attracted significant national attention, primarily because it's a novel idea, but mostly because we had a definite impact on the primary."*

After identifying interviews with *Ms* magazine and National Public Radio and referring to inquiries from Iowa, the National Women's Campaign Fund, and the Democratic Senatorial Campaign Committee, and the late attempt at replication by the Mondale-Ferraro campaign, Holstein continued:

> *"We believe we've been successful because this is a personal, independent group with diffused authority and shared responsibility — that's unlike any other campaign committee that women know about or read about — but what's more, it's unlike what women face every day in their jobs or, sometimes, in their homes."*

She then addressed the campaign itself:

> *"What is upsetting and offensive to the women in our group is the allegation that Joan has run a negative, or I believe the word was 'sleazy' campaign."*

And Holstein concluded:

> *"We believe this campaign is a role-reversal spurred by independent Minnesota women like the ones in our pyramid. . . . We've accomplished what we set out to do on August 9 and we believe we've put Joan Growe very, very close to the door of the U. S. Senate. . . . Hopefully, we can still put her inside too."*

Steering Committee members played reporters, asking a question or two, and then we folded our banner and slowly stole away. Oh, yes, we can say that we should have asked Joan Growe to be there even though we recognized that she had other priorities so close to the election, or that we should have hounded the press more, or that our announcement should have been more provocative. In any event, there was no news. It was a portent of things to come.

That same evening was the occasion of Growe's last fundraiser. It was held at the Nicollet Island Inn and Marofsky, Stuhler and West decided to have dinner beforehand. They were joined by Arvonne Fraser whom Stuhler encountered by chance because Fraser thought the event was earlier than it was. There was a lot of talk that night about the repercussions of a Reagan-Boschwitz win and its effect on women. We took some solace knowing how long it had taken for women to get the vote. The passage of the 19th amendment to the U. S. Constitution in 1920 required:

52 years of campaigning
480 efforts to get state legislatures to submit women's suffrage planks
277 campaigns to get state party conventions to include women's suffrage planks
47 campaigns to get state constitutional conventions to write women's suffrage into state constitutions
30 campaigns to get presidential party conventions to adopt women's suffrage planks into party platforms
19 successive campaigns with 19 successive Congresses

We predicted that we, the successors to the suffragists, would not give up, that the same passionate intensity that governed our forebears would also be our inheritance. Many years ago, Mildred Hargraves, a former President of the League of Women Voters of Minnesota, commenting on the seeming futility of achieving a legislative objective, noted that "it will require patience and longevity—we are women and we have both." It was with a positive sense of the inevitability of our ultimate success that we left the dinner table and joined Joan Growe's supporters.

The featured speaker (in this instance he chose poetry over prose) was Garrison Keillor, the popular host of Minnesota's Public Radio program, "Prairie Home Companion." Steering Committee members present applauded Keillor's wit and wisdom, but the realities of the polls took their toll in the conversations. The talk was not of victory. Even so, the final fund-raiser was a fitting cause for some later celebration because Growe raised more money than any other DFL candidate in the history of that party. She did not spend more because both Bob Short and Mark Dayton, previous senatorial candidates, drew on the their own personal fortunes to finance their campaigns. The Growe campaign raised $1.6 million. It was, according to one campaign worker, nearly enough. If more money had been available earlier, more could have been spent on radio and television to articulate Growe's positions on the issues. In the end, any positive images were diluted by the use of TV time to raise questions about the reasons for Boschwitz's failure to release his income tax returns, his support of the product liability legislation, and his seeming unwillingness to increase taxes to deal with the disturbing deficit. Hence, the positives about Joan Growe did not penetrate the consciousness of the voting public, and the negatives lingered on.[24]

Election day — Tuesday, November 6 — was beautiful, sunny and almost balmy for Minnesota at that time of year. Volunteers had been recruited by Growe headquarters to be poll watchers, to drive disabled or elderly voters to their polling places, and to perform a myriad of other related tasks. Although that request had been communicated through part of the pyramid by the two last-minute phone banks, we really did not press the matter. Jean West was the one member of the Steering Committee who took the day off (if you are your own boss, it's a bit easier to make those kinds of arrangements). She remembers in bewilderment one able-bodied man of 40 or so with no discernible disabilities whom she drove four blocks to the polls.

On election night, members of the Steering Committee of Minnesota's Groweing were invited to a Growe reception at the Minnesota Club. Downtown St. Paul was festive. The St. Paul Radisson Hotel, where the Mondale party was staying, displayed large and colorful banners, police cars lined the streets, and crowds were gathering. The final Mondale and Minnesota DFL rally was to be held at the St. Paul Civic Center, adjacent to the Minnesota Club.

The atmosphere inside the Club was subdued. The reception was a thank-you to the larger contributors, to friends

and family, to campaign workers, and to Minnesota's
Groweing. Barring a miracle, Joan Growe would *not* be
elected to the United States Senate.

Later that evening at the Civic Center, she made a gra-
cious concession speech. Rudy Boschwitz was elected to a
second term as U. S. Senator from Minnesota.[25] The vote
was 1,199,926 to 852,844. Boschwitz garnered 58 percent of
the vote, Growe 41 percent. The Minnesota turnout was
projected to be 2,130,000 or 70 percent of eligible voters.
The actual turnout was a bit less — 2,052,770 or 69.5
percent.[26]

In an analysis of the vote in the *St. Paul Pioneer Press* on
Thursday, November 8, Bill Salisbury wrote, "Women did
not flock to the polls in unusually large numbers to vote for
candidates Geraldine Ferraro and Joan Growe. But the
historic presence of those two women on the ballot sparked
large turn-outs of anti-feminist voters." His report was
based on the findings of the Northstar Election Profile, a
computerized election model of Minnesota voting
patterns — a model considered an accurate indicator of
statewide election trends. Salisbury's article noted that
"Anti-abortion voters appeared to be the most highly motivated. The largest turnouts were 84 percent in the precincts
identified as most staunchly fundamentalist in religion and
82 percent in predominantly Catholic districts. . . . Although Boschwitz is Jewish and Growe is Catholic, he out-
polled her two to one in the most staunchly Catholic precincts, and carried areas with large concentrations of
fundamentalist Christians by similar margins."

Growe carried only five counties — Carlton, St. Louis,
Lake, and Itasca in the Northeastern part of the state and
Mower in the Southeast. Mondale won Minnesota because
he added the populous counties of Anoka, Hennepin, and
Ramsey plus a few scattered counties in other parts of the
state.

Despite the dimensions of her defeat (but she did better
than any of the nine other women challengers for U. S. Sen-

ate seats), another article carried by the *St. Paul Pioneer Press* was introduced with the headline, "Growe is winner in women's cause." The news story quoted Growe as saying, "Even though we didn't win, we opened doors that will never be closed again. This was not the year that women won, but there's going to be a year for women in the future. I hope we provided some leadership and encouragement for those women." In the same article, Marilyn Bryant, a Republican activist, was quoted as saying, "The more women run, the more women are going to lose. But that's OK. These women ran extemely credible campaigns, and that's very exciting for women." Another Republican, Kris Sanda, former vice-chair of the Independent-Republican party said that the importance of Growe and Ferraro became clear to her in a recent conversation with her 24-year old daughter: "She said she had never pictured herself as a candidate for high office. But she said she wasn't going to think of herself as a volunteer any more." Later on Growe was quoted again, "Men and women have to allow women to be women in politics and not just honorary men. If women run a tough campaign, they're mean and shrill. If they raise the issue of human rights and social justice, they're viewed as naive." Bryant agreed that women are going to be subjected to the that double standard as long as it is still a novelty for women to seek those offices. "That's part of the package, and women know that. So we just have to dig in and fight harder."[27]

In a later article by Growe in a publication of the National Women's Political Caucus, she wrote:

> "A lot of the myths about women in politics will have to be rewritten now. The myths that exist — women can't raise enough money to run a campaign, women can't withstand the long hours required of a Senate candidate, women can't get the support and endorsement of all the groups necessary to put a campaign

together — they are all wrong! We did all those things, and we did them well."

But Growe also observed:

"We also learned that having a woman on the ticket does not automatically mean that a woman will vote for her. I think all women involved in politics, whether they were running for office or campaigning for a candidate, felt very proud. But that did not spill over to the general public in epidemic proportions. Many women put women candidates to a tougher test. We were not given the luxury of being able to afford even one mistake."[28]

Many analysts believe that Boschwitz was unbeatable. Others suggest that Growe's negative campaign was her downfall.[29] Still others are convinced that the Growe organization never fully tested the potential of what a woman candidate can achieve through grass-roots campaigning: greater emphasis on attending special events in communities even when there may be no media coverage; meeting with smaller groups with special concerns; having something to give away (Growe buttons and bumper stickers were in short supply); addressing more directly and completely the things that matter to most women. Of course, there have to be trade-offs. Women candidates cannot ignore either the media or the need for raising money. They have to learn to be better performers and less apprehensive about asking for money — big money. Growe did these things well. She held her own in the televised debates with her primary and general election opponents. She built an impressive campaign chest. Perhaps there was some measure of timidity that prevailed. Tradition is a very powerful force in politics and to defy tradition when one is already running at risk requires a significant departure from the norm. In her memoirs of the campaign, Geraldine Ferraro writes, "From the beginning there had been a mild division within the campaign about whether to position me as a national candidate with no single-issue platform — or to play up my gender by emphasizing women's issues." Ferraro says that her decision was an easy one — to be a vice presidential candidate of all the people. But as election day drew near, the Ferraro campaign changed tactics to go after the women's vote, and she did so in a series of speeches. Given the tenor of the political times, it is unlikely that a greater effort in this direction by either Ferraro or Growe would have changed the outcome. But there are women in Minnesota and elsewhere who believe that future women candidates seeking election to the House or Senate are going to have a better chance at success if they do those things that women do best and let tradition take the hindmost.[30]

Minnesota broke from the national pattern — narrowly — to give its vote to native son, Fritz Mondale. Otherwise, both Democrats and Republicans in the Minnesota Congressional delegation were all returned to office. The resistance to change also prevailed in Minnesota and gave incumbency the edge.

And then there was the extraordinary difference between people's positions on issues and their preferences for candidates. Obviously, Growe's pro-choice position hurt her. Her positions on full employment, equality, fair farm prices, a decent environment, excellence in education, and foreign policy — especially the arms race — did not persuade Minnesotans who generally are concerned with and support those issues. Growe, noting Boschwitz's massive spending on localized ads, direct mail, billboards, radio and television spots, remarked:

"That kind of media penetration explains how a senator can become reelected when he disagrees with the majority of Minnesotans on the need for a nuclear freeze, support for the ERA and the Civil Rights Act

of 1984, and the senselessness and immorality of nerve gas production."[31]

What about the gender gap? National exit polls showed less of a gap than anticipated. Men favored Reagan over Mondale by 63 percent to 36 percent. But women also favored Reagan, though by a smaller margin — 57 percent to 42 percent. The so-called women's issues — ERA, pro-choice, pay equity, a nuclear freeze, and remedies for the feminization of poverty — were not priorities on the agendas of most candidates and, consequently, not on the agendas of most voters. In Minnesota, however, it was a different story — 53 percent of Minnesota women voted for Mondale-Ferraro, only 45 percent for Reagan. Why the difference? The Twin Cities are widely regarded as one of the foremost feminist communities in the United States.[32] Minnesota was the first state to have a shelter for battered women. The Minnesota Women's Campaign Fund is a model for similar organizations around the country. Minnesota has been adept at networking and coalescing. While the Minnesota Women's Network (originally All the Good Old Girls) has its counterparts in other states, the role played by the Minnesota Women's Consortium with close to 130 member organizations may be unique. "At the Foot of the Mountain" is very likely the first women's theatre group. Minnesota is the first state to implement a plan of pay equity for its employees. These are but a few examples of the commitment to feminism in Minnesota which made the gender gap more of a factor here than was the case nationally. It is also interesting to note that although Growe did well in northeastern Minnesota where there was a lot of traditional male opposition to her candidacy, she benefited from party loyalty, a depressed economy, and the vigorous campaign she waged to win allegiance and get out the vote. Throughout the state, however, men favored Boschwitz by a large margin.

The funding gap was substantial. Although Growe raised a record amount of money for a DFL candidate, Boschwitz outspent her by nearly four to one ($5,890,445 to $1,578,720). At the campaign's end, Growe was nearly $45,000 in debt (that debt was finally paid off by year's end, 1985). Boschwitz still had close to $280,000 on hand. Growe received more than $1,000,000 in individual contributions, less than $500,000 from political action committees.[33]

But the most devastating effect was Mondale's close win in Minnesota. The national ticket gap that Ellen Goodman cautioned about two weeks before the election turned out to be true. Mondale barely carried Minnesota by 3,761 votes out of 2,114,842 votes cast. It was the final reality that could not be overcome in a contest with an incumbent, a Reagan Republican, and a man with overwhelming financial resources.[34]

For Growe herself, the most difficult thing about the whole campaign was the constant pressure. As a woman, she bore the burden of both public scrutiny and great expectations. "If I had failed in putting forth a good candidacy, in raising money, it would be that much more difficult for other women."[35] In a retrospective interview seven months after the election, Joan Growe commented, "The one thing I know for certain about where I am today as a politician and a person is that I'll never be frightened again. I've looked at the way I ran the race and what we were up against, and I don't think I could have run much harder or better and still be Joan Growe. . . . I feel good. You can lose, but in some very important ways you can feel you won something in how you got there." The interviewer noted, "Growe's satisfaction . . . was the self-respect with which she emerged from her effort and stubborn drive. Her campaign . . . was cause, ambition and adventure. As such it mattered to thousands of women."[36]

We are persuaded that Growe's campaign did matter to thousands of women, thousands who found an outlet for their commitment through Minnesota's Groweing. We were not, of course, the only expression for that commitment. Some could give money to the Growe campaign, and they did. Some played important roles in the campaign organization and others attended to the nitty-gritty. But for many women throughout the state, there was no other channel for their energy and enthusiasm until Minnesota's Groweing came along.

6 | The Evaluation

ALTHOUGH OURS WAS A MIXED record — a big win in the primary and a big loss in the general election — our overall assessment was positive. The Steering Committee spent several hours at Myrna Marofsky's on Saturday, November 17, 1984, evaluating the performance of Minnesota's Groweing.

The Mistakes We Made

The most critical mistake was our failure to be more specific about our need to pay off our note of $25,000. Our primary expenses were $25,120. The 150,000 buttons cost us the most — $16,000. Our total costs amounted to $26,981. We were not profligate but we made too much of a point that a button contribution should be voluntary so as not to prevent people from signing up for Growe. Actually, we know now that $1.00 was not, in most cases, a deterrent. We did receive $1.00 contributions even from those in low-income neighborhoods.

As we contemplated what we might have done, we realized that there was an alternative approach that could have: 1) lightened the paperwork; 2) simplified the pyramid reporting process; 3) provided an early warning on weaknesses in the organization, and 4) assured enough money to pay expenses as well as given us a known sum for general election efforts.

A contribution of $10.00 for each kit by each member of the Committee of 10,000 would have given us up-front money of $100,000 with an ample safety margin even if we did not receive a 100 percent return. Although that amount may have precluded some from participating, we are confident that they would have been few in number and that the recruiting task would not have suffered as a consequence. Every member of the Committee of 10,000 could then have decided whether or not to ask for the suggested contribution of $1.00 per button in order to recoup their $10.00 investment. The $10.00 would have been collected by the Committee of 1,000 when the kits were delivered. Ideally, those "bag ladies" would have sent us $100 as soon as they distributed their 10 kits. With such an arrangement, the money would have come in earlier and in larger amounts. We would also have known—if the money did not come in — where we might need some volunteer replacements. The 10, the 100, and the 1,000 also had kits and could have been asked for $10.00 as well. But $10.00 at those levels was less important than their primary responsibility of recruiting the next level of recruiters. The Committee of 10,000 were the key workers in this political vineyard.

Our initial lesson then was not that we spent too much money, but that we should have employed some device such as the one described above to get an initial return on our investment as we began the process rather than depending on the process itself to provide us with income to retire the debt.[1]

Our second mistake (and in some ways it is a serious contender for the number one spot) was not adequately involving the members of the Committee of 100 more fully in the process. Early on, each of the 10 on the Steering Committee should have met with each of her 10 on the Committee of

100. In this way, we could have instilled a sense of team work and perhaps even a spirit of competition — a prize (dinner with Growe?) to the team that got the most signatures. We could have done any number of things to give the Committee of 100 more of a feeling of ownership in the enterprise.

The Steering Committee could have benefited in a number of ways. We would have had an earlier and broader infusion of ideas. We could have called on all of them — not just a few — to help with the tedious and time-consuming activity of assembling all those materials into all of those kits. We could have had more helpers with other tasks — public relations, the preparation of materials, and so on. We would, had we so involved the Committee of 100, been enriched by a shared commitment. This is not to say that many of them were not committed to the same degree as the Steering Committee — they were. But we failed to put their talents to good use. Our one attempt to involve the 100 on September 4 was really too little and too late. We were operating under such stringent time pressures that we improvised and we did not delegate. Next time, we will know better.

Our third mistake could be called "great expectations." We expected that, even with occasional fissures in the pyramid structure, we would garner more signatures than we did and more money than we did. Ruby Hunt, an experienced politician, kept cautioning us that "you can't expect perfection in politics." Well, we didn't but we simply did not anticipate the magnitude of our shortfall. Martie Norton, also an old-hand at political campaigns, said at our evaluation meeting that she was aware that things might not come off in the way that we hoped, but everything was going so well at the Steering Committee level that she kept biting her tongue and not saying anything. She, too, was swept up in our mutual enthusiasm and hard work.

A fourth error or misjudgment may have been the decision to continue beyond primary day. Although our overall goal was Growe's election to the U.S. Senate, Minnesota's Groweing came into existence because we were determined that the experience of other DFL-endorsed candidates in losing primary contests would not befall Growe. We should probably have stopped with the primary victory. We were not able to establish a new mission for the general election, and, consequently, we lost both energy and momentum. But we could not resist the pressures. Time and again we heard, "Minnesota's Groweing is the only thing that can save the Growe campaign." We were not at all certain that was the case as, of course, it proved not to be. Nevertheless, we would have felt some guilt in not extending our efforts, in not giving whatever else we might have been able to contribute to the ultimate outcome. Minnesota's Groweing remained the single channel where ordinary people could give themselves — not just money — to the Growe campaign.

There was another critical constraint on our effectiveness — time. If we had gotten together earlier, we could have prepared a budget earlier than we did, we could have organized regional extensions of the pyramid in communities throughout the state, we could have refined and simplified the materials, we could have arranged for a phone — maybe even an office — as well as a P. O. Box. (West was quoted in *Ms* magazine as having said "we were a pyramid without a desert to sit on.")[2]

The list of "should-haves" or "could-haves" goes on and on. But the constraints of time are also endemic to political campaigns. Without that sense of urgency, we might not have accomplished as much as we did. Nonetheless, we were well aware of our shortcomings.

The Good Things We Did

Our mistakes are not the whole story of Minnesota's Groweing.

We believe we were successful because, as Linda Holstein said in the press conference when nobody came, "this is a personal, independent group with diffused authority and shared responsibility." We were different from other campaign commitees and, for that matter, different from a lot of other kinds of organizations. We were all leaders, all involved, all committed to a single goal. There was no chair as such; there was never even talk of any officers except that, by law, we had to have a treasurer. Because of her prior experience as a campaign manager and her knowledge of Federal Election Commission requirements, Myrna Marofsky got the nod, and her name appeared on all our materials.

It was fitting that the Minnesota's Groweing Steering Committee functioned in the way that it did. We rejected, however subtly, the male hierarchial tradition — we did it "our way," and it worked. Each member brought a somewhat different perspective or talent to the organization. As a matter of fact, it was an extraordinary coincidence that 10 women brought together in a rather casual way coalesced so effectively. Few of us knew all the others well if at all — there were some exceptions — so the socialization process was important. We enjoyed each other, we liked each other, we laughed a lot even when we were stuffing kits, certainly not high on anyone's list of a really fun thing to do. We were women as friends — or becoming friends — working for a common goal. Minnesota's Groweing demonstrated what women organized and committed can contribute to a political campaign. Mary Kay Blakely in her *Ms* magazine article, "From Minnesota: Recipe for Homemade Revolution," described her meeting with the Steering Committee, "I caught a glimpse of the electric energy they shared."[3]

Rosabeth Moss Kanter has written that "Power is the ability to *do*, in the classic usage of power as energy." We mobilized resources to get a task done. In that context, Minnesota's Groweing demonstrated that power, as Ellen Goodman has said, need not be dominating and hostile but instead creative and sustaining. It was creative and sustaining by virtue of both our mission and our process. Other levels of the pyramid were empowered — they controlled the way in which they went about the business of recruiting their 10 or signing up their 10 (or 20) voters for Growe. When more people are empowered, more gets done. If there was any not-so-secret formula to our success, this was it.[4]

It would be impossible to estimate the thousands of individual and collective hours we spent in this activity. We reached out to 283 communities (not counting the Twin Cities and their suburbs). Minnesota's Groweing buttons could be found in the tiny hamlets of Barnesville, Isle, Milroy, and many, many more. We became a visible presence in the effort to put Joan Growe into the U. S. Senate.

The political environment was a help. Minnesota's Groweing was created in what was a good year for women in American politics. Geraldine Ferraro became the first woman vice presidential nominee on a major party ticket. Joan Growe, after a strenuous contest, received the DFL party's nomination for U. S. Senator on the 19th ballot. It was in that climate that Minnesota's Groweing was able to recruit so many willing women workers so quickly. Success followed success with Growe's primary win over Mattson. The Ferraro rally was another significant recognition. Minnesota's Groweing was riding a high.

There were other achievements. We had a non-partisan cast; we were not part of the official Growe campaign, and we signed up Independents and Republicans, as well as Democrats, who pledged a vote for Growe. We are confident that we involved people who had never before been politically active. We got their commitment. Finally, it must be said that in these days of media campaigns, we proved that grass-roots' campaigns still have political significance and relevance. That same sense of "what can we do?" that motivated the founders of Minnesota's Groweing was experienced by other women's groups around the country. But as Maureen Dowd wrote in a *New York Times*

Magazine article, "Amid increasing tension with the Mondale men, women's groups tried to mobilize the troops, but with campaign funds pouring into the media and polls rather than into grass-roots organizing, the groups could scarcely find what they now scathingly call 'the phantom campaign.' " Dowd quotes Linda Davidoff, chair of Women for Mondale-Ferraro in New York as saying, "and then they found out to their frustration — we must've gotten the comment 500 times — nothing is happening out there."[5]

If imitation is the sincerest form of flattery, then we have more reason to be proud of our achievements. Not only did the Ferraro-Mondale campaign in Iowa follow suit, the national campaign also made a last ditch effort to create a pyramid with a 25-person base.[6] In the last calls from Growe headquarters, voters were urged to go to the polls and call 10 others with the same reminder and request.

In the final analysis, then, Minnesota's Groweing did some things wrong and some things right. We did not put Joan Growe into the United State Senate, but we were, we believe, instrumental in achieving Growe's impressive victory over Bob Mattson in the primary election. In doing so, we involved myriads of Minnesotans in the political process. We were not ingrown — rather we reached out to women new to politics who now may find themselves with a life-long enthusiasm or commitment. Minnesota's Groweing was an ambitious and gutsy undertaking, and nothing can ever take away from its organizers the pride we feel and the joy we experienced. The answer to "Are you havin' any fun?" was "you bet." We are convinced that this model can be adapted for other women's campaigns, that it is a "way to go." There is no sense of failure among us because we did demonstrate what women whose energy and enthusiasm can be enlisted in a good cause can do. We are pleased that Joan Growe spoke of us with respect and appreciation, "I can't say enough about the 10 women who organized Minnesota's Groweing — they were effective, efficient, and energizing."[7] While we have no doubts that women's campaigns need to be run differently, we do not mean to reject the need for either the polls or the media but rather to add a dimension that reflects the "differentness" that most women bring to politics. Minnesota's Groweing provided that dimension in Joan Growe's campaign for the U.S. Senate and, with all our shortcomings, we are proud that someone wrote of us, "[Joan Growe's] bid for the U. S. Senate mobilized an amazing 'Minnesota's Groweing' campaign that brought her closest of any Democratic woman Senatorial candidate to victory in 1984."[8] Like Joan Growe who said of her decision to run for the United States Senate, "I have no regrets," we, too, have no regrets about the time and effort we invested in the organization of Minnesota's Groweing. We will remember it as a highlight of our political lives.

Afterword

A FAITHFUL STAFF MEMBER called my 1984 U.S. Senate Campaign "a race against the odds." In politics, as in life, I guard myself against false optimism. Real disappointment is keen enough without adding to it unnecessarily. I did not run my race to lose. I did not run just to raise issues. I ran because I believed, and still do, that I would have made a positive difference as a U.S. Senator.

As I look back on the year 1984 — despite my loss — I savor many victories. As one headline said after the election: "Joan Growe: Beaten but not Defeated."

First was the victory of the endorsement against three credible male opponents. It may have taken 19 ballots and 26 hours, but we did it, having led on every single ballot. Second was a smashing 76 percent primary victory. Two months earlier, you could have gotten good money that I would not survive a primary, let alone earn a landslide victory.

Our success in raising money was another victory. We raised more money than any other Democrat in the history of Minnesota, including Hubert H. Humphrey and Walter F. Mondale. That victory was possible because of the belief of many, especially women, that we were right on the is-

sues. We received contributions — many of them under
$5 — from 22,001 individuals, from young and old alike.

Finally, there was the victory of meeting thousands of
supporters throughout the state and, indeed, throughout
the country. Women from all walks of life and work were
eager and willing to help, and their enthusiasm gave me the
strength to keep going. A case in point was Minnesota's
Groweing, an organization started by a small group of
women concerned with issues important to all women —
and whose dedication to me I will never forget. Their particular approach was a creative and innovative way to involve citizens — both men and women — in the political
process.

As each day passes, I take even greater pride in the standards we raised. We said military spending must be
reduced. We said that the arms race could be put to rest if
we stopped building and testing new nuclear weapons. We
said that diplomacy, not force, is the first requisite for a
more peaceful, humane, and democratic world. In all these
assertions we were assailed as dangerous and naive. Will
history prove us right? Of course it will.

We predicted that Social Security would be under attack.
We argued that the solution to the farm crisis demanded not
just more loans, but fair prices and profits for farmers. I
continue to think we are right. We said the tax system was
a fraud crying for reform and, today, reform is high on the
agenda of the opposition party.

We maintained that education is the best investment in
our future. We asserted that the answer to our devastating
deficit was not just economic growth but a tax increase on
the wealthiest of Americans who often pay less than their
fair share.

We campaigned for equal rights, comparable pay, and
the Civil Rights Act of 1984. We asked for expansion and extension of the Superfund to clean up the toxic wastes. We
faced the fact that three out of the four who are poor are

women and children and by the year 2000, if that trend continues, the only poor would be women and children.

On the fundamental question of human rights, we insisted that no one's rights are protected unless everyone's rights are secure. We warned of a nation divided, rich from poor, black from white, male from female, those enjoying tax cuts from those sustaining life with governmental surplus cheese. That was not the country I envisioned growing up in rural Minnesota. That was not the nation for which I raised my children. That was not the kind of society I would have promoted in the U.S. Senate.

Minnesota, I believed, was a special place where great and wondrous and new things could happen. It was the home of pioneers. And in the modern age, it was my quest to be a new pioneer. It was not the destiny for me in 1984, to be sure, but in other ways, we set out to make a difference—and we did!

There was so much life, so much heart—even tears—in my campaign. The contest was against the odds, but the experience was liberating and filled with the warmth of eager supporters and cherished workers. With a week remaining of the campaign, I was cheered as I crossed a bridge from North Dakota (the site of the nearest airport) to a town in northern Minnesota. The temperature was far below freezing. The hour was late. I knew that the race was lost. But that memory of cheering Minnesotans in the north country is alive and lasting.

I recall two other moments with a special fondness. Following a televised debate, fathers brought their daughters to me to sign the program. Another time—at a senior citizens picnic—an older woman took me aside and said, "Joan, keep after them, we've got a lot of pride in you." Those memories, too, will be a source of continuing strength, filled, as they were with hope and love.

Political observers continue to marvel at my buoyancy and good feeling following my defeat. They expected devastation and bitterness. Oh, there was sadness — but no regrets.

Five times I have run for office. Four times I have won. I learned more in defeat than in all of the victories combined. Once renewed, I may try again. In the meantime, I will lend my support to those who carry on.

As I said in my concession speech, "I began my campaign by quoting Robert Kennedy. He said that every time a person stands up for an ideal, a tiny ripple of hope is sent forth that will one day become a wave; a wave that would break down the mightiest walls of oppression and resistance. For all our mothers, and for all our daughters, a journey has ended, but the wave has begun."

Although we did not win, we opened doors that will never be closed again. 1984 was not the year women won, but there is going to be a year for women in the future. I hope I provided some leadership for those women. I look back with pride, and forward with hope. I am optimistic once again.

Joan Anderson Growe

Notes

Preface

1. On March 30, 1985, Cathy Long (D. LA) was elected to fill the seat left vacant by her husband, bringing to 23 the total number of women in the House of Representatives. *Women's Political Times*, A Publication of the National Women's Political Caucus, May/June 1985, Vol. X, No. 2.

2. *Women in State Government.* Fact Sheet from the Center for the American Woman and Politics, Rutgers University, New Brunswick, N. J., January 1985. (In addition to the 11 elected secretaries of state, six other women serve in that capacity by virtue of appointment.) On Tuesday, November 5, 1985, Mary Sue Terry was elected Attorney General of Virginia by a margin of 22 percent over her opponent. Her fellow Democrats who ran for Governor and Lieutenant Governor were elected by margins of 10 percent and 4 percent respectively. *The New York Times*, November 7, 1985.

3. *Christian Science Monitor*, December 14, 1984.

4. Ruth B. Mandel, Director of the Center for the American Woman and Politics, to the Minnesota Women's Campaign Fund, June 20, 1985.

5. A post-election study, "Women as Candidates in the 1984 Congressional Elections," done by Cooper and Secrest Associates for the National Women's Political Caucus revealed the positive effect of Geraldine Ferraro's candidacy: 27 percent of the voters polled said they would be more likely to support a woman for public office; only 7 percent said they were less likely to do so. In addition, they found that women are perceived more positively than men on 7 of 10 measures of personal and profes-

sional stereotypes – being caring, being effective, having strong opinions, having new ideas, fighting for their beliefs, understanding the needs of voters and speaking directly to the point. Women are judged equal to men on having leadership qualities and on inspiring confidence. The single characteristic on which women were stereotyped negatively compared to men is the ability to handle a crisis. In those districts where there were both male and female candidates running, voters gave the women significantly higher marks on six of eight additional stereotypes: better able to understand the voters' personal views; having more concern about war and peace issues; being more likely to work hard; having stronger personal convictions; being more honest, and having more compassion for needy people. The women were rated equally with the men on being prepared to speak about major issues and lower on the ability to handle the emotional demands of public life. *Women's Political Times*, A publication of the National Women's Political Caucus, Vol. X, No. 1, January-February 1985.

6. Black women are also making gains. They constitute 22 percent of all black elected officials. In 1984, there were "significant firsts." Roxanne Jones of Philadelphia – Pennsylvania's first black woman state senator. Yvonne Miller of Norfolk – first black woman since reconstruction to be elected to the Virginia House of Delegates. Margaret Carter of Portland – first black woman in the state legislature. Jo Celeste Pettway – Alabama's first black female judge. *Washington Post National Weekly Edition*, June 24, 1985.

7. Gloria Steinem, "What No One Else Would Tell You About the Ferraro Campaign, *Ms*, December 1984, p. 70.

Chapter 1. The Setting

1. *Minnesota*, University of Minnesota Alumni Association, May/June 1985, p. 41.

2. Speech by Joan Growe to the Women's Economic Roundtable, Minneapolis Club, March 13, 1985.

3. *Ibid.*

4. *Minnesota*, p. 41.

5. Dulcie Lawrence, *Minneapolis Star and Tribune*, June 2, 1982; *Minneapolis Star and Tribune*, June 7, 1982; *St. Paul Pioneer Press*, June 7, 1982.

6. Marlene Johnson was founder and owner of an advertising agency called Split Infinitive. She had been a key figure in the organization of the National Women's Political Caucus and the National Association of Women Business Owners.

7. *The Minnesota Legislative Manual 1982–83: State of Minnesota.* Compiled by Joan Anderson Growe, Secretary of State.

8. Elaine Voss to Barbara Stuhler, October 10, 1985.

9. *St. Paul Pioneer Press*, October 3, 1983.

10. Interview of Andrea Christianson by the author, October 16, 1985.

11. *The Gender Gap 1984: How Women Will Decide the Next Election.* (Boston: Houghton Mifflin, 1984).

12. *Minneapolis Tribune*, March 22, 1984.

13. *St. Paul Sunday Pioneer Press*, June 17, 1984.

14. June 16, 1984.

15. However impressive and exhausting, this was not the longest ballot count in DFL history. In 1966, Lieutenant Governor A.M. (Sandy) Keith won the endorsement over incumbent Karl F. Rolvaag on the 21st ballot at the state convention in the Leamington Hotel in Minneapolis. Rolvaag went on to challenge the nomination by entering the primary election which he won. However, he lost the general election to Republican Harold LeVander. For a detailed account of this fascinating episode in Minnesota politics, see David Lebedoff, *The 21st Ballot: A Political Party Struggle in Minnesota*, Minneapolis: University of Minnesota Press, 1969.

16. *St. Paul Pioneer Press*, June 18, 1984.

17. Andrea Christianson interview, October 16, 1985.

18. *St. Paul Pioneer Press*, June 18, 1984.

19. Andrea Christianson interview, October 16, 1985.

20. Prior to the state DFL convention, the strategy team consisted of Growe; Andrea Christianson, Caucus Coordinator; Carol Faricy, Finance; Bob Meek, Press Consultant, and Elaine Voss, Deputy Secretary of State (information from Elaine Voss, October 14, 1985).

21. *Minneapolis Star and Tribune*, July 6, 1984.

22. *Minneapolis Star and Tribune*, July 2, 1984.

23. *St. Paul Pioneer Press*, July 4, 1984.

24. Robert Mattson was elected state auditor in 1974 and lost that position to R. Arne Carlson in 1978. He ran unsuccessfully for state auditor in 1970 and for the 4th district Congressional seat in 1976. (*Minneapolis Star and Tribune*, September 12, 1984).

25. *St. Paul Dispatch*, September 12, 1984.

26. June 19, 1984.

27. Data on elections taken from *Minnesota Legislative Manuals, 1966–66, 1979–80*, Compiled by the Secretary of State.

28. *St. Paul Pioneer Press*, July 7, 1984.

29. *Minneapolis Star and Tribune*, July 2, 1984.

30. In 1922, Anna Dickie Oleson ran as the Democratic candidate for the U.S. Senate but the party was then not a major force in Minnesota

politics. The Republican and Farmer-Labor parties were the dominent
political forces in the state. The Senators were Knute Nelson (Rep.) and
Henrik Shipstead (Farmer-Labor) who defeated Frank B. Kellogg, the
Republican incumbent in the 1922 election. Oleson came in a poor third.
Representatives included eight Republicans, one Independent, and one
Farmer-Laborite. The Governor, J.A.O. Preus, was also a Republican.
Interestingly, that same year, Susie W. Stageberg ran as the Farmer-
Labor candidate for Secretary of State, and while she came in second behind the popular Republican incumbent, Mike Holm, she was far ahead
of the Democratic candidate. (*Legislative Manual of the State of Minnesota*. Compiled for the Legislature of 1923 by Mike Holm, Secretary
of State.) Ultimately, Mike Holm's wife — Virginia Holm — was appointed to succeed her husband in 1952 as Secretary of State, the first
woman in Minnesota history to hold that office. She was then elected in
her own right for a two-year term in 1954. (*Caucus*, Newsletter of the
Minnesota Women's Educational Council, May 1985, p. 4.)

31. *Minneapolis Star and Tribune*, July 17, 1984.

32. A Minnesota Poll reported that 28 percent of Minnesotans would
be more likely to vote for Mondale because of Ferraro — men 21 percent
and women 35 percent. (*Minneapolis Star and Tribune*, July 20, 1984.)

33. *St. Paul Pioneer Press*, July 1, 1984.

34. Arvonne Fraser to Barbara Stuhler, October 8, 1985.

35. *St. Paul Pioneer Press*, July 1, 1984.

Chapter 3. The Beginning

1. In August 1983 when prospects of a Growe entry into the 1984
Senate race were approaching reality, Martie Norton, Yvette Oldendorf,
Emily Anne Staples, and Mary Vogel-Heffernan met with Bob Meek and
Elaine Voss to express their views on the forthcoming campaign. They
knew that any candidate — male or female — brings both strengths and
weaknesses into the political arena. Their attempts to point out the
strengths of a woman in both the substance and process of a campaign
were received — or so they sensed — in a patronizing way by Bob Meek.
Nearly a year later, they were still concerned.

2. Andrea Christianson interview, October 16, 1985.

3. The Minnesota Women's Campaign Fund is a multipartisan organization designed to raise money for the purpose of supporting progres-
sive women candidates who meet the Fund's criteria. Three of the
twenty-five directors — Kathleen Scott, Barbara Stuhler, and Jean
West — were later to become members of the Steering Committee of Minnesota's Groweing.

4. Arvonne Fraser to Barbara Stuhler, October 8, 1985.

Chapter 4. The Organization

1. Although the Bylaws of the Minneapolis Club were changed in 1977, the first woman member did not join in her own right until 1978.

2. Actually 11 women were at the breakfast. Andrea Christianson from the Growe campaign headquarters joined us. Even though we were an independent political campaign group and thus had to be very careful not to do anthing giving the appearance of unlawful collaboration, it was appropriate that the Growe organization know about our existence and be aware of what we intended to do.

3. "Are You Havin' Any Fun?" Music by Sammy Fain; Lyrics by Jack Yellen, 1939.

4. After the primary the Democratic Senatorial Campaign Committee gave $241,000 to the Growe campaign. According to a prior agreement, the Committee spent the money to purchase media time for the Growe campaign (Elaine Voss to Barbara Stuhler, October 10, 1985).

Chapter 5. The Outcome

1. *St. Paul Dispatch*, September 12, 1984.

2. *Ibid.*

3. September 2, 1984.

4. Elden Kirsch quoted in the *St. Paul Dispatch*, September 12, 1984.

5. *Minneapolis Star and Tribune*, September 9, 1984.

6. Materials from the office of the Secretary of State.

7. September 8, 1984.

8. September 12, 1984.

9. September 13, 1984.

10. *The Minnesota Legislative Manual 1981–82: State of Minnesota*, Compiled by Joan Anderson Growe, Secretary of State.

11. *Legislative Manual 1979–80.* The other five contenders were Sal Carbone (American Party of Minnesota), Bill Peterson (Socialist Worker), Leonard Richards (Libertarian Party), Jean T. Brust (Workers Party), and Brian J. Coyle (Public Interest Independent).

12. Geri Joseph in a conversation with Barbara Stuhler, August 28, 1984.

13. *Ibid.*

14. Lori Sturdevant in the *Minneapolis Star and Tribune*, September 8, 1984.

15. Several versions of the proposed Uniform Product Liability Act have been introduced into the Senate since 1982. Senator Ernest F. Hollings (D.-S.C.) has described the measure as "the snake oil of our day," claiming that it is "anti-consumer" and "probably unconstitutional." Paul

Broduer, "Annals of Law: The Asbestos Industry on Trial," Part IV, *The New Yorker*, July 1, 1985, p. 79–80.

16. *St. Paul Pioneer Press*, July 15, 1984.

17. *Minneapolis Star and Tribune*, October 30, 1984.

18. *St. Paul Pioneer Press*, July 13, 1984.

19. Tom Borman, a Minneapolis attorney who raised substantial funds for the Mondale campaign, made a special effort to ensure that Ferraro's aides were put in touch with Minnesota's Groweing. During a phone conversation with Steering Committee member Linda Holstein less than a week before the September 19th rally, Borman broached the idea that Joan Growe should also benefit from the publicity surrounding Ferraro's visit to Minnesota. He suggested that Minnesota's Groweing was a natural vehicle for organizing the rally, and Holstein agreed. The fund-raiser was not for Growe, as the Growe campaign had hoped, but for the Mondale-Ferraro ticket voter registration drive.

20. *St. Paul Dispatch*, September 20, 1984.

21. *Ms*, December 1984, Vol. XIII, No. 6, p. 56.

22. *St. Paul Dispatch*, September 18, 1984.

23. *Minneapolis Star and Tribune*, July 28, 1984.

24. B.J. Mahling in a conversation with Barbara Stuhler, November 1, 1984.

25. In a private letter sent to 22 Republican Senators up for reelection in 1986 and subsequently published in the *Wall Street Journal*, Boschwitzh shared the secrets of his success. They should, he wrote, disregard media criticism of large financial contributions, give few speeches, discourage debates, don't release tax returns, walk — don't ride — in parades, and "Stop every 100 yards and conspicuously wipe the sweat off your brow." Growe took umbrage at his cynicism, "The Boschwitz campaign had nothing to with public policy, public issues." (*St. Paul Pioneer Press and Dispatch*, May 2, 1985. Reinforcing that view was the comment of Wyman Spano, a knowledgeable observer of Minnesota politics, "Joan Growe lost because Rudy Boschwitz is a lot like Ronald Reagan: People like him and vote for him without thinking much about his policies." (Quoted in *Citybusiness*, December 5.18, 1984, p. 33).

26. Information from the office of the Secretary of State.

27. November 8, 1984.

28. *Women's Political Times*, Vol. IX, No. 7, November/December 1984.

29. Bill Salisbury in the *St. Paul Pioneer Press*, November 8, 1984.

30. Geraldine A. Ferraro (with Linda Bird Franke), *Ferraro: My Story*, New York: Bantam Books, 1985, p. 312.

31. *Women's Political Times*, November/December 1984.

32. Conversation of several Steering Committee members with Mary Kay Blakely, contributing editor of *Ms* magazine, September 11, 1984.

33. *St. Paul Pioneer Press*, December 8, 1984. State Senator Steven Novak, Growe's campaign manager, commented that Growe would have raised more money had it not been for Mondale's efforts in Minnesota which he estimated cost her $250,000 and the Jewish community's support of Boschwitz's pro-Israel position which cost her an additional several hundred thousand dollars. (*Ibid.*)

34. Information from the office of the Secretary of State.

35. Joan Growe in a speech to the Women's Economic Roundtable, Minneapolis Club, March 13, 1985.

36. Jim Klobuchar, *Minneapolis Star and Tribune*, June 9, 1985.

Chapter 6. The Evaluation

1. The debt was greatly reduced by two post-election benefits. Deborah Bancroft, a member of the Committee of 100, hosted a "Going Out of Business Sale" on March 2, 1985, and Ramsey County Commissioners Diane Ahrens and Ruby Hunt (also a Steering Committee member) hosted a "Final Debt Reduction" on June 4, 1985. The debt was finally retired on December 31, 1985.

2. Mary Kay Blakely, "From Minnesota: Recipe for Homemade Revolution (A Personal Trip to the Twin Cities Where Trends are Born), *Ms*, July 1985, p. 57.

3. *Ibid.*

4. Rosabeth Moss Kanter, *Men and Women of the Corporation.* New York: Basic Books, Inc., 1977, p. 166. Ellen Goodman, *Minneapolis Tribune*, April 11, 1976.

5. The *New York Times Magazine*, December 30, 1984. In the same article, Minnesota's Lieutenant Governor, Marlene Johnson, is quoted as saying, "In this particular election, women were ignored." This statement demonstrates again the concern of feminists that a different strategy should have been employed to exploit the historical status of the Vice Presidential candidate. It was the same point that Minnesota women were making about the Growe campaign.

6. In a September 24, 1984 letter to Julia Moore at Mondale-Ferraro headquarters in Des Moines, Jean West reported:

"There is no way we can possibly assess how much of a factor Minnesota's Groweing was in Joan Growe's success. We suspect that we did contribute in significant measure. We had a large number of people throughout the state who involved men and women in the

pyramid who had never before been part of the political process. We also motivated persons who might have been indifferent about the primary to get out and vote."

7. Joan Growe in a speech before the Women's Economic Roundtable, Minneapolis Club, March 13, 1985.

8. Blakely, "From Minnesota", p. 110.

Appendices

A. Chronology of major events and meetings.

B. Map showing location of communities outside the Twin Cities metropolitan area with Minnesota's Groweing participants.

C. List of communities outside the Twin Cities metropolitan area participating in the Minnesota's Groweing pyramid.

D. Committee of 100.

E. Initial communication to the Committee of 100 (memo, checklist, calendar).

F. Press release announcing the formation of Minnesota's Groweing.

G. Memo to the Committee of 1,000.

H. Committee of 1,000 timetable.

I. Memo to the Committee of 10,000 (printed on envelope containing kit materials).

J. Information sheet on Joan Growe.

K. Sample signature sheet.

L. The button.

M. The postcard.

N. The supporting cast.

A. Chronology of Major Events and Meetings

Saturday July 14, 1984	Meeting at Martie Norton's on the St. Croix
Wednesday July 18	Breakfast at the Minneapolis Club
Wednesday July 18	Meeting at Mary Vogel-Heffernan's
Saturday July 21	Meeting at Emily Anne Staples'
Tuesday July 24	Luncheon meeting at Ruby Hunt's
Wednesday July 25	Meeting at Stuhler/West residence
Friday July 27	First batch of Minnesota's Groweing buttons (West to Twin Cities airport)
Monday July 30	Meeting at Stuhler/West's
Tuesday July 21	Second West airport run for buttons
Wednesday July 22	Third West airport run for buttons
Thursday August 2	Fourth West airport run for buttons
Tuesday, July 31 through Tuesday August 8	Materials, kits, and buttons assembled into 1,110 shopping bags

Wednesday August 8	Breakfast meeting at the Normandy Hotel
Thursday August 9	Kickoff breakfast at the Prom Center
Wednesday August 22	Meeting at Stuhler/West's
Tuesday August 28	Meeting at Stuhler/West's
Saturday September 1	Hunt, Stuhler and West at the Farmer's Market
Tuesday September 4	Reception at Campus Club for Committee of 100 Steering Committee dinner meeting at Grandma's
Tuesday September 11	Primary election day Dinner meeting with Mary Kay Blakely of *Ms.*
Wednesday September 12	Meeting at Stuhler/West's
Saturday September 15	Stuhler/West/Lynn Christianson site tour for Ferraro rally
Sunday September 16	West with Ferraro rally advance workers
Wednesday September 19	Ferraro rally Ferraro reception
Tuesday September 25	Meeting at Stuhler/West's
Sunday October 21	Meeting at Stuhler/West's

Monday October 22	Meeting at Stuhler/West's
Monday October 29	Phone bank
Tuesday October 30	Interview by National Public Radio
Tuesday November 6	Election day!
Saturday November 17	Evaluation meeting at Marofsky's
Wednesday December 12	Breakfast meeting at the Normandy on the deficit
Thursday February 14, 1985	Breakfast meeting at the Normandy on the deficit (plans for the Bancroft benefit)
Saturday March 2	Bancroft benefit "Going Out Of Business" sale
Thursday May 2	Breakfast meeting at Ruby Hunt's (plans for the Ahrens/Hunt benefit)
Tuesday June 4	Ahrens/Hunt "Final Debt Reduction"

B. Map Showing Location of Communities Outside the Twin Cities Metropolitan Area with Minnesota's Groweing Participants

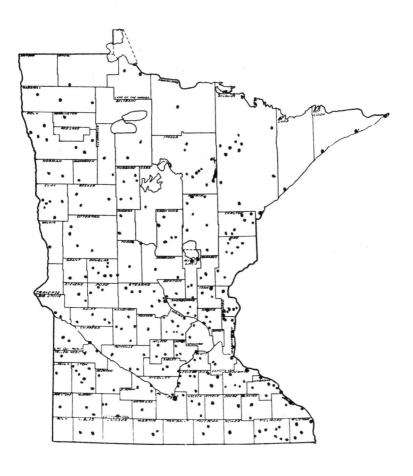

C. List of Communities Outside the Twin Cities Metropolitan Area Participating in the Minnesota's Groweing Pyramid

ADA	BROWNTON	DETROIT LAKES
ADRIAN	BRUNO	DILWORTH
AFTON	BUFFALO	DULUTH
AITKIN	BUFFALO LAKE	E. GRAND FORKS
ALBERT LEA	CALEDONIA	ELK RIVER
ALEXANDRIA	CALLAWAY	ELY
ANGORA	CAMBRIDGE	ERHARD
ANOKA	CANBY	ERSKINE
APPLETON	CANNON FALLS	ESKO
ARLINGTON	CANTON	EUCLID
ASKOV	CARLOS	EVANSVILLE
ATWATER	CARLTON	EVELETH
AUSTIN	CEDAR	FAIRFAX
AVON	CENTER CITY	FAIRMONT
BACKUS	CHISHOLM	FARIBAULT
BAGLEY	CLARKFIELD	FARMINGTON
BARNESVILLE	CLARKS GROVE	FERGUS FALLS
BARNUM	CLEAR LAKE	FINLAYSON
BAUDETTE	CLITHERALL	FISHER
BAYPORT	CLOQUET	FOLEY
BELLE PLAINE	COHASSET	FOREST LAKE
BEMIDJI	COKATO	FORESTON
BENSON	COLD SPRING	FOSSTON
BETHEL	COLERAINE	FRANKLIN
BIG FALLS	CORRELL	FULDA
BIGFORK	COTTONWOOD	GARFIELD
BIG LAKE	CROOKSTON	GAYLORD
BLAINE	CROSBY	GHENT
BOVEY	CROSS LAKE	GLENCOE
BRAHAM	CYRUS	GLENWOOD
BRAINERD	DAKOTA	GLYNDON
BRECKENRIDGE	DALBO	GOODHUE
BRIMSON	DAWSON	GOODLAND
BROOK PARK	DEERWOOD	GRANADA
BROOKSTON	DELANO	GRAND MARAIS

GRAND PORTAGE	LOWRY	NORTHFIELD
GRAND RAPIDS	LYND	NORWOOD
GRANITE FALLS	MABEL	ODESSA
GRYGLA	MADISON	OGILVIE
GUTHRIE	MADISON LAKE	ONAMIA
HAMBURG	MANKATO	ORTONVILLE
HANCOCK	MANTORVILLE	OSAGE
HARMONY	MAPLE LAKE	OSAKIS
HASTINGS	MAPLE PLAIN	OSTRANDER
HAWLEY	MARCELL	OWATONNA
HENDERSON	MARINE on the	PALISADE
HENDRICKS	ST. CROIX	PARK RAPIDS
HERMAN	MARSHALL	PELICAN RAPIDS
HIBBING	McGRATH	PENNOCK
HILL CITY	McGREGOR	PEQUOT LAKES
HINES	MELROSE	PINE CITY
HOFFMAN	MENAHGA	PINE ISLAND
HOUSTON	MILACA	PIPESTONE
HUTCHINSON	MILROY	PLAINVIEW
ISLE	MILTONA	PRINCETON
JACOBSON	MINNEISKA	PRIOR LAKE
JANESVILLE	MINNEOTA	RED WING
JORDAN	MINNESOTA CITY	RENVILLE
KASOTA	MONTEVIDEO	ROCHESTER
KELLOGG	MONTGOMERY	ROGERS
KENYON	MONTICELLO	RUSH CITY
KERKHOVEN	MONTROSE	SABIN
KERRICK	MOORHEAD	SARTELL
KETTLE RIVER	MOOSE LAKE	SAUK CENTRE
LA CRESCENT	MORA	SAUK RAPIDS
LAKE CITY	MORRIS	SCANDIA
LAKE GEORGE	MOTLEY	SEARLES
LAKE ITASCA	MOUNTAIN IRON	SHAFER
LAKE LILLIAN	MURDOCK	SHAKOPEE
LAKEVILLE	NASHWAUK	SIDE LAKE
LAMBERTON	NELSON	SILICA
LANESBORO	NEVIS	SLAYTON
LAPORTE	NEW GERMANY	SLEEPY EYE
LE SUEUR	NEW LONDON	SOUTH HAVEN
LEXINGTON	NEW PRAGUE	SPRING GROVE
LINDSTROM	NEW RICHLAND	SPRING VALLEY
LITCHFIELD	NEW ULM	ST. ANTHONY
LITTLE FALLS	NEWFOLDEN	ST. CLOUD
LONG PRAIRIE	NORTH MANKATO	ST. JAMES

ST. JOSEPH
ST. PETER
STACY
STAPLES
STEPHEN
STEWARTVILLE
STILLWATER
STOCKTON
STORDEN
STRATHCONA
STURGEON LAKE
SWATARA
TACONITE
TAUNTON
THIEF RIVER
   FALLS

TOFTE
TRACY
TRAIL
TWIN VALLEY
TWO HARBORS
VIRGINIA
WABASHA
WADENA
WANAMINGO
WARBA
WASECA
WATERTOWN
WATERVILLE
WAUBUN
WAVERLY
WEAVER

WEBSTER
WESTBROOK
WHALAN
WILLIAMS
WILLMAR
WILLOW RIVER
WINDOM
WINONA
WORTHINGTON
WRENSHALL
WYKOFF
WYOMING
ZIMMERMAN
ZUMBRO FALLS
ZUMBROTA

D. Committee of 100

Rosemary Ahmann, Rochester
Jean Albrightson, Minneapolis
Barbara Amram, Minneapolis
Pat Anderson, Golden Valley
Mary K. Bachman, Minneapolis
Jane Binder, Minneapolis
Lynn Bolnick, St. Louis Park
Christine Cammack, St. Paul
Joan Campbell, Minneapolis
Mary Cannon, St. Paul
Marge Christensen, St. Paul
Elizabeth Clark, Inver Grove
   Heights
Kathleen Cota, Minneapolis
Carol Daly, New Hope
Cheryl Dickson, St. Paul
Janet Dieterich, St. Paul
Kay Elliasen, Golden Valley
Nancy Evans, Hastings
Bridget Faricy, St. Paul
Eleanor S. Fenton, St. Paul
Marion Fogarty, Belle Plaine
Diane E. Follmer, St. Paul
Ruth Frederick, Duluth
Judith Gaston, Minneapolis
Gloria Gebhard, St. Paul
Sally Graven, Minneapolis
Florrie Gray, Minneapolis
Gloria Griffin, Tonka Bay
Mary Hartmann, St. Paul
Ellen Hartnett, St. Paul
Ellen Hendin, Minnetonka
Diane Hendrickson, Min-
   neapolis
Carolyn Hiatt, Bloomington
Molly Hoban, St. Paul
Lucinda Jesson, St. Paul
Ellen Johnson, St. Paul
Alice Keller, Winona
Marcia Keller, Minneapolis
Monika Kiley, Orono
Edie Lallier, St. Paul
Peggy Lucas, Minneapolis
Naomi Lyon, Minneapolis
Catherine Mathison, Fridley
Shirley Maxwell, Plymouth
Pat McCart, St. Paul
Sue McCloskey, St. Paul
Grace McGinnis, Minneapolis

Patti McInroy, Minneapolis
Eileen McMahon, St. Paul
Chris Merritt, Golden Valley
Christine Meuers, Minneapolis
Lisa Miller, St. Paul
Sue Moravec, Crystal
Gladys Morton, St. Paul
Edith Mucke, Edina
Katherine Murphy, Wayzata
Mary Lou Nelson, Minneapolis
Barbara Nemer, Minneapolis
Kathryn Nickles, Golden Valley
Luanne Nyberg, Minneapolis
Pat O'Connor, St. Paul
Claire T. Olson, Edina
Debra Page, Minneapolis
Medora Perlman, Minneapolis
Sandra Peterson, New Hope
Martha Platt, Minneapolis
Jane Preston, White Bear Lake
Jeri Rasmussen, Shoreview
Kit Reynolds, Minneapolis
Isabel Rife, White Bear Lake
Sue Rockne, Zumbrota
Elaine Saline, St. Paul
Mimi Sands, Aitken
Susan Sands, St. Paul
Dorothy Scanlan, St. Paul
Miriam Seltzer, Minneapolis
Sandra Shearer, St. Paul
Sandy Skaar, St. Paul
Elin Skinner, St. Paul
Norma Sommerdorf, St. Paul
Peggy Specktor, Golden Valley
Margo Stark, Minneapolis
Mary Stringer, St. Paul
Kathy Tatone, Edina
Janabelle Taylor, St. Paul
Joane Vail, White Bear Lake
Evelyn Van Allen, St. Paul
Sharon Rice Vaughn, St. Paul
Diane Vosick, Golden Valley
Sally Walls, Minneapolis
Lynn Ward, St. Paul
Julie Belle White, St. Paul
Lorraine Wood, St. Paul
Shelley Wright, St. Paul
Lois Yellowthunder, St. Paul

E. Initial Communication to the Committee of 100 (memo, checklist, calendar)

YOUR PYRAMID CONTACT IS:

MINNESOTA'S GROWEING 100,000

July 25, 1984

TO: THE COMMITTEE OF 100

FROM: THE STEERING COMMITTEE (Virginia Greenman, Linda Holstein, Ruby Hunt, Myrna Marofsky, Martha Norton, Kathleen Scott, Emily Anne Staples, Barbara Stuhler, Mary Vogel-Heffernan, Jean M. West)

Congratulations for being willing to take this bold step with us! You are now part of MINNESOTA'S GROWEING, an independent, grassroots organization that will demonstrate the effectiveness and power of women by electing Joan Growe to the U.S. Senate.

We have asked you - the Committee of 100 - to form the Committee of 1,000.

The Committee of 1,000 in turn will form the Committee of 10,000 - which will be the group that will be asked to recruit 100,000 Grove voters in the September 11 Primary.

In order to achieve this result in the Primary, we must move swiftly and efficiently. We are counting on you and asking you to follow this timetable:

AUGUST 1
1. Report the names of the 10 women you are recruiting to your pyramid contact (noted above). Send her your list of names, including addresses and phone numbers and tell her how many of your 10 will be attending the MINNESOTA'S GROWEING breakfast (Joan will be there) on Thursday, August 9 at the Prom Center, 1190 University Ave. W., St. Paul at 7:30 A.M. (Cost - $5.00).

AUGUST 9
2. Deliver the materials which will be available at the breakfast to any of your 10 volunteers who are unable to be there that morning.

AUGUST 16
3. Call your 10 to remind them of their deadline to get their 10 names to you.

AUGUST 20
4. Get those names in the mail to your pyramid contact.

AUG 23, 30
5. Call your 10 again to remind them to call their 10 volunteers if they have not yet received back a completed signature sheet.

SEPTEMBER 7
6. Call for the last time - the most important call of all - to have them call their volunteers reminding them to get in the signature sheets and to phone each of the names on their copy of the signature sheet to make sure those voters get to the Primary.

The telephone is the crucial link in the MINNESOTA GROWEING campaign to have Joan win big on September 11. We know that you will stick with us and demonstrate that women organized CAN MAKE A DIFFERENCE! Keeping in touch with your 10 on the designated dates to remind them to do the same with their 10 will help us discover any weak links that need attention.

A calendar as well as a checklist is enclosed for your convenience.

YOU CAN PUT JOAN GROWE IN THE UNITED STATES SENATE

Prepared and paid for by MINNESOTA'S GROWEING, Myrna Marofsky, Treasurer

YOUR PYRAMID CONTACT IS _____

Phone_____

THE COMMITTEE OF
100
CHECKLIST

THE COMMITTEE OF 1,000	WILL ATTEND THE 7/9 BREAKFAST	RECEIVED MATERIALS 7/9 or ?	CALL TO REMIND OF 8/17 DEADLINE	10 NAMES RECEIVED & SENT TO CONTACT	PROGRESS CALL	PROGRESS CALL	GET OUT THE VOTE CALL
	√	√	8/16	√	8/23	8/30	9/7
PHONE #							
PHONE #							
PHONE #							
PHONE #							
PHONE #							
PHONE #							
PHONE #							
PHONE #							
PHONE #							
PHONE #							
PHONE #							

JULY

			18 7:30 am Mpls. Club **FIRST MEETING OF STEERING COMMITTEE**	19	20	21
22	23	24	25	26 Mail in your 10 names as soon as you can to your pyramid contact	27	28
29	30 Your pyramid contact will be getting nervous and will call you!	31				

AUGUST

			1 DEADLINE to send names of your 10 to contact w/breakfast reservations	2	3	4
5	6	7	8	9 7:30 A.M. BREAKFAST Prom Center 1190 University Ave. W. St. Paul	10 Deliver the materials to any of your 10 who did not attend breakfast	11
12	13	14	15	16 Call your 10 to remind them of their 8/17 deadline for their 10 names	17 DEADLINE for your 10 to get their 10 names to you. (the names of the Committee of 10,000)	18
19	20 YOUR DEADLINE for getting the 10 sets of names to your pyramid contact.	21	22	23 Call your 10 to remind them to call their 10 to get signature sheets in soon!	24	25
26	27	28	29	30 Call to repeat message above - TIME IS NOW SHORT	31	

SEPTEMBER

						1
2	3	4	5	6 ONE LAST CALL to remind all to call the "signatures" to get to the 9/11 polls	7	8
9	10	11 **PRIMARY** Overwhelming SUCCESS! thanks to your efforts	The Committee of 10,000 will be asked to return any leftover materials to their Committee of 1,000 contact who will be asked to get the accumulated extra supplies to you. We would like a final return date from you of September 25.			

F. Press Release Announcing the Formation of Minnesota's Groweing

---

MINNESOTA'S GROWEING

August   , 1984

FOR IMMEDIATE RELEASE

FROM: Steering Committee, Minnesota's Groweing

Contact: Emily Anne Staples   (O) 612 473-0221
                                  (H) 473-9120

          Jean M. West   (O) 612-224-6211
                                   (H) 612-224-4516

A new organization to recruit 100,000 voters for Joan Growe in the Minnesota primary on September 11 was formed by a group of 10 women representing a wide range of civic interests and concerns. According to one of the organizers, Virginia Greenman of St. Paul, "We have developed a pyramid structure, beginning with the original 10, each of whom has recruited another 10 women and they, in turn, still another 10. We now have 1,000 women who will sign up 10,000 men and women who will then seek the signatures of 100,000 Minnesotans who will pledge their vote for Joan Growe on September 11."

The response has been "extraordinary," according to Emily Anne Staples of Plymouth. "It demonstrates," she said, "the eagerness of women of Minnesota to put their energies to work for Growe as the new U.S. Senator from Minnesota.

Each voter who signs up for Growe will receive a numbered MINNESOTA'S GROWEING button. Joan Growe will be presented with button number one and on the day before the Primary, she will receive button number 100,001. The numbers in between will be worn by voters who will have pledged their votes to Growe.

A kick-off breakfast is being held in St. Paul's Prom Center on Thursday, August 9, at 7:30 a.m. On that occasion, the nucleus of the 1,000 volunteers recruited by MINNESOTA'S GROWEING will hear from their candidate and then go about the business of finding 100,000 men and women who will vote for Growe in the September 11 primary.

This is a spontaneous, grass-roots movement led by women who believe they can make a difference in the political landscape of this State. "It is that difference," said Jean M. West of St. Paul, "that can put Joan Growe in the United States Senate."

Members of the Steering Committee include: Virginia Greenman, St. Paul; Linda L. Holstein, Minneapolis; Ruby Hunt, St. Paul; Myrna Marofsky, Plymouth; Martha Norton, St. Paul; Kathleen Scott, St. Paul; Emily Anne Staples, Plymouth; Barbara Stuhler, St. Paul; Mary Vogel-Hefferman, St. Paul; Jean M. West, St. Paul.

G. Memo to the Committee of 1,000

YOUR PYRAMID CONTACT IS:

August 7, 1984

TO: The Committee of 1000

FROM: The Steering Committee (Virginia Greenman, Linda Holstein, Ruby Hunt, Myrna
Marofsky, Martha Norton, Kathleen Scott, Emily Anne Staples, Barbara Stuhler,
Mary Vogel-Heffernan, Jean M. West)

Thank you for your help and commitment. You are now part of MINNESOTA'S GROWEING,
an independent, grass-roots organization that will demonstrate the effectiveness and
power of women by electing Joan Growe to the U.S. Senate. Three weeks ago, ten women
met for breakfast and formed the steering committee which in turn organized the Committee
of 100.

You have been asked by a member of the Committee of 100 to be a member of the Committee
of 1,000 that forms the Committee of 10,000. This will be the all-important group
that will go about the business of recruiting 100,000 Growe voters in the September 11
Primary.

In order to achieve this result, we must move swiftly and efficiently. We are counting
on you and asking you to follow this timetable:

August 9-16 1. Recruit your 10 volunteers - men and women - and give each one
a kit from the shopping bag you received at the August 9 breakfast or, if you could not attend, was subsequently given to you
by your pyramid contact (noted above).

August 17 2. Report the names, addresses, and phone numbers of your volunteers
to your pyramid contact.

August 24, 31 3. Phone your 10 volunteers and ask them for progress reports
(remember: they have been instructed to keep the pink copy
for calling and to send the yellow copy to you. You, in turn,
should send those yellow copies to your pyramid contact).

August 9-31 4. Use the kit prepared for you (also in the shopping bag):

° to get your own list of signatures.

° to send your signature sheet(s) to MINNESOTA'S GROWEING,
P. O. Box 75700, St. Paul, MN 55101, sending the yellow
copy to your pyramid contact and saving the pink copy to
call your names prior to the Primary.

° to distribute, as your volunteers request them, the 35 extra
buttons and Growe information sheets as well as the 10 extra
signature pages.

Sept. 8-10 5. Call your 10 volunteers to remind them of the Primary on Sept. 11
and ask them to call those they signed up (from their pink sheet(s),
reminding them to be sure to vote.

The telephone is the crucial link. Keep in touch with your 10 volunteers on the
designated dates. We know that you will stick with us and demonstrate that women
organized **CAN MAKE A DIFFERENCE!**

A timetable is enclosed for your use in tracking your 10 volunteers.

YOU CAN PUT JOAN GROWE IN THE UNITED STATES SENATE

Prepared and paid for by the MINNESOTA'S GROWEING Committee, Myrna Marofsky, Treasurer

H. Committee of 1,000 Timetable

YOUR PYRAMID CONTACT IS _____

Phone _____

THE COMMITTEE OF 1000 TIMETABLE	Recruit volunteers and deliver kits	Report names, etc. to contact	Progress calls	Collect and send in signature sheets	Get out the vote call
THE COMMITTEE OF 10,000	8/9-16	8/17	8/24 & 8/31	8/17-9/10	9/8-9/10
Phone #					
Phone #					
Phone #					
Phone #					
Phone #					
Phone #					
Phone #					
Phone #					
Phone #					
Phone #					
Phone #					
Phone #					

MINNESOTA'S GROWEING 100,000

I. Memo to the Committee of 10,000 (printed on envelope containing kit materials)

YOUR PYRAMID CONTACT IS: _____

Address _____

Telephone _____

TO: **THE COMMITTEE OF 10,000**

MINNESOTA'S GROWEING is a grass-roots campaign to have Joan Growe win big in the September 11 Primary. You are essential to making it happen.

YOU ARE THE VOLUNTEERS WHO WILL BE RECRUITING 100,000 GROWE VOTERS!

In order to achieve this result for the Primary, we are asking you to:

1. Examine the contents of your kit which includes 2 signature pages (in triplicate), 10 numbered buttons and 10 information sheets on Joan Growe.

2. Get 10 people to sign the signature sheet (don't forget yourself), and as soon as 10 signatures have been obtained, follow the instructions at the bottom of the sheet.

3. Give each person who signs up for Growe a numbered button and an information sheet. Suggest that the sheet can be given to others who may be asking questions about Joan Growe.

4. Ask each potential signer the following:

   a) have you already signed a pledge to vote for Growe? (obviously we want to avoid duplicates)

   b) are you a registered voter? (If not, remind them that they can register at the polling place on Primary day)

   c) will you wear your numbered Growe button as often as possible?

   d) will you give a $1.00 donation for the button? (this is important in order to cover our expenses, but we do not want to eliminate anyone who cannot make a donation)

5. Be sure that the information is clearly recorded on the signature page and the two copies. (no carbons are needed)

6. Keep the pink copy so that within one or two days prior to the September 11 Primary you can call those who signed to remind them of their commitments to vote for Joan Growe.

7. Use the second signature page if you feel that you can get more than 10 names. We hope you can! (Additional buttons and Growe information sheets are available from your pyramid contact.)

8. Return the white original and the donations to **MINNESOTA'S GROWEING**, P.O. Box 75700, St. Paul, MN 55101 and make sure you get the yellow copy to your pyramid contact as soon as possible.

We appreciate your help in this campaign. We know that you will stick with us and demonstrate that **MINNESOTA GROWEING**, a people-not-dollars organization, **CAN MAKE A DIFFERENCE!**

YOU CAN PUT JOAN GROWE IN THE UNITED STATES SENATE

Prepared and paid for by **MINNESOTA'S GROWEING**, Myrna Marofsky, Treasurer. P.O. Box 75700, St. Paul, MN 55101

J. Information Sheet on Joan Growe

MINNESOTA'S **GROWEING** 100,000

YOU CAN PUT JOAN GROWE IN THE UNITED STATES SENATE.

If anyone should ask, "Why should I make a special effort to vote for Joan Growe in the Primary on September 11 — is it really that important?" tell them:

- if Joan loses in the Primary, there is no tomorrow.
- if Joan has only a modest victory in the Primary, there will be little enthusiasm or little money coming her way for the general election contest with Rudy Boschwitz.
- conservative Republicans are likely to mount a cross-over campaign and vote for Bob Mattson and against Joan in the DFL primary because Growe is seen by Republicans as the most viable candidate the Democrats could choose.

IN SHORT, IT IS VITAL THAT JOAN WINS BIG IN SEPTEMBER!

If anyone should ask, "What could Joan Growe bring to the U.S. Senate?" tell them:

- hard work, high ideals, the ability to mobilize others to action.
- experience as a teacher, legislator, and Secretary of State (remember that neither of the two incumbent U.S. Senators from Minnesota had any prior experience in public office).

If anyone should ask, "What does Joan Growe stand for?" tell them:

- **peace** — restraint of the arms race; talks with the Soviet Union; diplomacy — not force — in the high tension of Central America and the Middle East.
- **equality of opportunity** — the Equal Rights Amendment and other measures designed to reduce discrimination wherever it may exist, against whomever it may exist.
- **a decent environment** — policies attacking the problem of acid rain and the disposal of hazardous waste, assuring clean air and clean water.
- **a quality education** — achieving excellence in the classroom by giving teachers the salaries and status reflecting their worth.
- **a fair shake for farmers, workers, and consumers** — improve the country's economic performance by reducing the federal deficit, by changing the tax burden, by addressing continuing problems of industry and agriculture with new ideas and new policies.

These, of course, are simply short-hand expressions, lacking specifics, but they say something about Joan Growe's values and ideas. We know her vision is widely shared.

YOU CAN PUT JOAN GROWE IN THE UNITED STATES SENATE.

Prepared and paid for by the MINNESOTA'S GROWEING Committee, Myrna Marofsky, Treasurer, P.O. Box 75700, St. Paul, MN 55101.

K. Sample Signature Sheet

MINNESOTA'S GROWEING — AND I WILL VOTE FOR JOAN GROWE IN THE PRIMARY ON SEPT. 11

BUTTON #	NAME (please print)	STREET ADDRESS/CITY/ZIP	TELEPHONE	SIGNATURE	DONATION
69844	Linda Mueller	2310 NE 3rd St Apt5 55418	789-3920	(signature)	$1.00
69840	David W. Carlson	1116 Central Ave, Red W., 9 55066	388-2619	David W. Carlson	$1.00
69841	Donita King	1801 Lakewood Albert Lea, MN 56007	507- 373-5036	Donita King	1.00
69842	Cindy Gilbert	207 Bancroft Dr Albert Lea MN 56007	507- 373-3447	Cindy Gilbert	1.00
69543	Rev Marie Hardy	1606 Frank Hill Dr Albert Lea MN 56007	313-9684	Rev Marie Hardy	1.00
69845	CARROLL PACOLT	421 S.E. 10th Ave Faribault MN 55021	507- 334-2007	Carroll M. Pacolt	$1.00
69846	Margaret Jensen	1413 Gratiann Rd Qebert Lea, MN 55021 589	590-1007	Margaret Jensen	1.00
69847	Sharon Whitlow	420 Allen Ave Owatonna Minn	507 455-2381	Sharon Whitlow	1.00
69848	Phyllis Mae Johnson	1283 Randall Street Winona MN 55987	507 452-3410	(signature)	1.00
69849	Leonora Christensen	535 Harriet Lane Albert Lea MN 56007	507 373-4856	Leonora Christensen	1.00

BE SURE THIS FORM IS FILLED OUT COMPLETELY . . . ENCOURAGE A DONATION OF $1.00 OR MORE PER BUTTON (OPTIONAL)

Mail ORIGINAL and the donations to: MINNESOTA'S GROWEING
P. O. Box 75700
St. Paul, MN 55101

Send YELLOW copy to: Your Pyramid Contact.
Retain PINK copy for pre-primary calling

MINNESOTA'S GROWEING 100,000

Name of Recruiter _____ (please sign even though your name appears above)

Recruiter's Pyramid Contact _____

L. The Button

M. The Postcard

MINNESOTA'S GROWEING
P.O. Box 75700
St. Paul, Minnesota 55101

**REMEMBER TO VOTE FOR
JOAN GROWE ON NOVEMBER 6**
Your vote will make a difference

PLACE
13 CENT
STAMP
HERE

Prepared and paid for by the Minnesota's Groweing Committee, Myrna Marofsky, Treas., P.O. Box 75700, St. Paul, MN 55101

S-66

N. The Supporting Cast

Important supporting roles in the Minnesota's Groweing drama were played by a variety of persons of all ages who provided materials and services of all kinds. They deserve to be recognized. In alphabetical order, they are:

Al Edwards — the deliverer of the first batch of LarLu Line buttons in his own car from Winona to Jean West in her car near the airport.

Jim Gardner — owner of the Finch Building (before its sale in 1985) where the materials were assembled.

Benjamin Kehoe — three-month old son of Molly Greenman (one of the assembly line volunteers) was an especially happy diversion for all the assemblers who took occasional breaks to enjoy the pleasure of his company.

Jerry McCarthy — owner of the Chase Printing Co. which printed the Minnesota's Groweing materials.

Steve McGovern — the truck driver who provided the tool that opened the helium gas tank to fill the balloons for the inaugural event of Minnesota's Groweing in the Prom Center.

Will Stoltzman, Dave Tricket, Bill and Craig Lang — all of Winona Printing, the printers of the Minnesota's Groweing buttons.

Steve Styba — our contact at LarLu Line in Winona, the supplier of our buttons.

Gary Woelke — the accommodating banker at First Bank St. Paul

Linda Wood — a graphic designer who did the Minnesota's Groweing postcards.

Diane Yamish — a graphic designer who chose the color for the buttons.

And, finally, all those men and women (mostly teen-agers) who sorted and counted buttons (in order of quantity — from top to bottom):

Jay Heffernan   *Peggy Jones*
Matt Heffernan   *Bridget Faricy*
Mike Heffernan   *Amy Garcia*
Melissa Nelson   *Bridget McCafferty*
John Nelson   *Kelly Otte*
Carla Nelson   *David Bowman*
Rachel Nelson   *Mike Andert*
Edward West   *Melody Martagon*
Kim Otte   *Collen Hasley*

Index

Fundraising for Minnesota's Groweing
Nicollet Island Inn, 68–69
post-election benefits, 97 n.1
St. Paul Athletic Club, 61–62
totals, 70

Gardner, Jim, 119
Gender gap, 75
Goodman, Ellen, 60, 76, 83–84
Goseholt, Nancy, 50
Grass-roots campaigning, benefits
of, 73
Greenman, Virginia
founds Ramsey Women's
Political Caucus, 21
lobbying at MEA convention, 65
personal background, 15–16
at precinct caucus, 7
recalls Growe's Prom Center
speech, 48
role in founding Minnesota's
Groweing, 24, 26
Gregg, Ruth, 16
Growe, Joan
article on election campaign,
72–73
attends Democratic National
Convention, 12
on campaign issues, 88–89
campaign tactics criticized,
66–67
concession speech, 71
on convention strategy team, 93
n.20
counties carried in election, 71
defeats Mattson in primary, 53
dimensions of defeat, 71–72
on endorsement victory, 87
enters primary, 11
on fundraising efforts, 87–88
impact on politics, xvi
information sheet on, 115
on Minnesota's Groweing, 88
Minnesota House seat, 3–4
Nicollet Island Inn fundraiser,
68–69

personal life, 3–4
recalls election campaign, 76–77
reluctance to accept en-
dorsemennt, 8–10
as Secretary of State, 4
significance of candidacy on
women's politics, xxiii
speech at Prom Center
breakfast, 48–49
U.S. Senate candidacy, 5–6
on women's impact on politics,
89–90
Gun control, 53

Hargraves, Mildred, 69
Hartnett, Ellen, 63, 65
Hively, Jan, 24
Hollings, Ernest F. (Sen.), 95 n.15
Holm, Mike, 94 n.30
Holm, Shirley, 50
Holm, Virginia, 94 n.30
Holstein, Linda L.
Committee of 100 candidates, 39
Ferraro rally, 61–62, 96 n.19
on impact of Minnesota's Groweing, 67–68
lobbying at MEA convention,
65
National Public Radio interview,
66
on organizational strengths of
Minnesota's Groweing, 83
personal background, 16–17
recalls early Steering Committee
meetings, 37
recalls Minneapolis Club
meeting, 29–32
Humphrey, Hubert H., stature in
Minnesota politics, ix, 57
Humphrey, Hubert H. (Skip), 8
Hunt, Ruby
on financial problems, 97 n.1
grassroots campaigning skills,
38–39
lobbying at MEA convention, 65
personal background, 17
shopping bags, 45–46